Adding

VALUE
to Marketing

The Role of MARKETING

in Today's PROFIT-DRIVEN

ORGANIZATION

DAVID   P   DOYLE

**KOGAN
PAGE**

YOURS TO HAVE AND TO HOLD
BUT NOT TO COPY

First published in 1998

Kogan Page Limited
120 Pentonville Road
London N1 9JN

British Library Cataloguing in Publication Data
A CIP record for this book is available from the British Library.
ISBN 0 7494 2175 4

Typeset by Kogan Page
Printed and bound by Biddles Ltd, Guildford and King's Lynn

This book is dedicated to my daughters,
Marie-Astrid and Constance.

It is no use having a wonderful vision for the next century if you don't have the product right next week.

(Statement by Sir Richard Greenbury, Chairman, Marks and Spencer, in an interview in the *Financial Times*, 16 February 1998)

Contents

SOME WORDS OF INTRODUCTION

The inspiration to write this book arose from reading a stream of articles in financial newspapers, management and business journals, and in various research reports, on marketing -related related topics. Much of the material touched on the basis of my concerns regarding the changing marketing environment: the inertia in recognizing the shifting customer base away from youth to older client segments, increasing new product failures in the marketplace, higher costs associated with marketing activities, the pitfalls of using IT in marketing, the insular role of marketing in organizations *et al.*

It seemed to me that marketing, as a traditional function and dynamic business process, had somehow lost its way since I first started studying the subject at business school in the early 1970s. Few professionals will deny that the current marketing environment is more complex compared to the 1970s; fewer again would even recognize the changes that have taken place since the 1950s. Traditional markets are fragmenting as the customer base ages, increasing numbers of women participate in the workforce and birth rates remain stagnant in the developed world. At the same time, competition becomes relentlessly more acute as barriers to international trade are dismantled; a once distant player you may have associated with France, Hong Kong or Hungary is now capable of operating in your indigenous market; national frontiers no longer represent an impediment in generating sales. As the Internet inexorably penetrates traditional sales channel structures in certain markets, marketers can now reach potential clients across vast surfaces of the globe at considerably less cost.

What has corporate marketing done in the face of these developments? One would have thought the most obvious: respond with a thorough re-assessment of its strengths and weaknesses. This might have been accompanied by a move to get to grips with new opportunities and threats in the marketplace and devise appropriate cost-effective and more sharply-targeted marketing programmes

Research and other documented material – some from credible sources such as McKinsey management consultants – did little to imbue me with the impression that marketing was addressing these fundamental issues. Marketing seems to be locked in a time warp belonging to an era when conceptually attractive and manageable notions of the '4 Ps' were valid and the prime markets were young baby-boomers. But times have moved on.

Without pretending to provide a panacea or be in anyway prescriptive (although at times it was difficult to resist the temptation), these challenges continue to require serious reflection. I have started by highlighting the now well documented problems facing marketing: changing demographics, time dispersing acquisitions, poor costing mechanisms and an ossified perspective of the marketing mix, encapsulated in the original definition of the '4 Ps'. From there, I go on to propose some broad guidelines in tackling these issues.

The message is that in spite of improved productivity brought about by IT, a wider choice of media and the existence of barrier-free markets, a marketing approach that continues to promote mass-marketing and increasing variations of products, aimed at 'young' markets, is doomed to failure. Compounding this is the timid adoption of financial analytical tools to measure the cost and revenue streams associated with various market segments, product groups and elaborate marketing campaigns. Adding more product variations to increasingly fragmented markets is not a way forward, particularly if the cost element is ignored. Cost control becomes an unrewarding occupation and the quality of earnings suffers in the long term.

The ensuing chapters try to deal with some of these issues in a pragmatic fashion, drawing on research and studies carried out across the developed economies. Many of the techniques and suggested remedies have been around for some time and do not pretend to be in any way innovative. But the compelling feature is the use of multi-disciplines not necessarily associated with marketing operations, such as management accounting and behavioural science.

Perhaps one of the most important points to emerge from these chapters is the need to 'de-limit' marketing activities from its straight jacket and make it *the business* of everyone in the corporation. Marketing needs to be a multidisciplinary effort based on teams of people from all departments organized around customer relationships. But measuring the success of a marketing programme should be based not only on customer-focused concerns alone. My modest contribution to the debate on improving marketing is to suggest that corporate effort, and resources, should also be market-driven and capable of delivering sustainable cashflows, and, ultimately, improved profits.

Marketing that is obsessed with customer-satisfaction for its own sake is misdirected and resource wasteful. The bottom line has to shift to identifying and retaining customer groups that stay with the company in the long run, and who contribute to profitability on a sustainable basis.

David P Doyle
Paris, June 1998

1

Adding Value to Marketing - The Challenge

As the Millennium looms ahead, corporations are finding themselves facing challenges in the marketplace that may no longer be resolved by working harder on the same policies from the past, albeit with incremental adjustments, and supported by isolated organizational processes to sustain customer loyalty. Many of the shortcomings facing organizations could be best encapsulated by the perennial story of the chief executive who launches a simulated business game within his company to cultivate a more results-oriented culture. Executives duly form themselves into teams from each functional department – human resources, marketing, production and finance – to compete in separate groups in the simulated game, which is followed by a tangible profit target set by the CEO.

The outcome has a predictably familiar tone. The marketing people focus on sales and promotional activities. This results in an impressive market share but haemorrhages the enterprise of cash resources in the process. The finance team, obsessed with the bottom line, restricts investments earmarked for production and promotion. While safeguarding the cash position, no new products or upgradings are foreseen, leading to a slow death of the enterprise. The production team focuses on improving the manufacturing process and new product development. The result is the development of first-class products at the right price but insufficient resources for promotion and market development and thus an inadequate customer base. The human resources' team meanwhile concentrate on restructuring the organization and spend funds on training. Since they manage to retain more of the simulated enterprise's funds than the other teams, they win the game outright.

This tale does not conclusively prove that functional teams with similar perspectives are ill equipped to run a business or that *ad hoc* cross-functional teams are any more effective. It does, however, point to the fundamental misguided principle followed by senior management in pursuing business growth with outdated definitions of the customer base, serviced by organizational structures so compartmentalized and functionally insular that customer development gets missed out in the rush to optimize each unit's own results. Yet, attempts to cultivate an integrated and holistic customer-oriented structure, where each unit contributes to the continuous process of creation, delivery and sustaining of customer satisfaction, has produced little beyond ephemeral results. Servicing customers requires an organization-wide approach with the complicity of everyone, from the switchboard operator to the delivery staff. Being consumer-conscious is no longer enough if large parts of the organization continue to handle tasks that bear no relationship to the external customer and perform their tasks in an isolated fashion.

To be sure, obsession with cost-cutting during the 1990s did not create the ideal conditions for generating a more cross-functional culture within organizations; each department understandably focused available energy on protecting its own turf. While most functions were affected by the downsizing mode, the productivity-driven effort rarely led to a major rethinking or restructuring of the marketing activity. Any enhanced efficiency brought about within the marketing function through streamlining, outsourcing and other cost-containment measures obviously helped, but has rarely proven to be a long-term substitute for improved customer loyalty and sustainable income streams.

DISINTEGRATION OF CUSTOMER SERVICE

Compounding these phenomena has been the debilitating impact of management's failure to understand the process-driven approach in the consumer service value-chain; as long as organizations remain rigid structures divided by functional compartments into marketing, sales, production, finance – key core processes such as product development or simply customer-delivery fulfilment will continue to be treated on a piecemeal basis. Customer satisfaction, and ultimately customer retention, suffers if overlapping responsibilities in the order cycle (see Table 1.1), and the lack of timely management involvement, results in confusion, delays and complaints.

Table 1.1 *The customer-satisfaction chain: everyone is involved, but not in an integrated fashion*

Tasks	Department involved	Customer involvement
Sales planning	Marketing and sales	
Order-seeking	Sales	Receives a salesperson and listens to sales arguments
Order- cost estimates and negotiation of delivery dates	Sales, production and logistics	Awaits outcome
Order-taking and receipt	Sales and customer service	Agrees to order
Order-processing	Customer service	Awaits delivery
Production or processing scheduling	Production or operations	Awaits delivery
Order delivery	Logistics and accounts	Receives delivery
Invoices despatched	Accounts	Payment
Installation difficulties	Customer service Sales	Contacts with various units or within the company
Errors in order	Engineering, accounts	
Order rectified	Customer service, Accounts and logistics	?

Compartmentalized structures contribute to important customer-related issues such as answering enquiries being stalled between functional boundaries. Further along the chain, customers end up paying the cost for the inefficiencies in terms of late deliveries, mislabelled orders, inadequate sales advice and delayed after-sales service. Customers are the first to express dismay when simple routine requests for assistance by telephone go unanswered because of 'dis-integration' of internal services. The marketing function, which should operate as an integrated service, is managed independently by different departments – sometimes in perfect isolation – despite evidence suggesting that an integrated approach has a real and lasting value.

Transformation of companies into process-driven entities – focused on enhanced customer value-chains and a holistic approach to customer handling has largely remained elusive. A significant contributing factor in the eyes of some management experts has been the mysterious aura associated for too long with the marketing function, little understood and unwilling to integrate knowledge and skills from other parts of the organization.

Growing discontent with the inertia of marketing departments is now rising to the surface. Management thinkers now refer to the 'mid-life crisis' of marketing and argue that it must take the lead in reinventing itself. McKinsey, the management consultancy group, in its highly critical report of 1993 on the marketing function, summarized the views of many senior managers in the first paragraph:

> Whatever the reality behind marketing's vaunted contribution to corporate success, the large budgets it has enjoyed for decades are finally beginning to attract attention – even criticism. So much so, in fact that doubts are surfacing about the very basis of contemporary marketing: the value of ever more costly brand advertising, which often dwells on seemingly irrelevant points of difference; of promotions, which are often just a fancy name for price cutting; and of large marketing departments, which, far from being an asset, are often a millstone around an organization's neck.

THE BUDGET PROCESS – TOO MUCH REVERENCE TO THE PAST

The one organizational process that might have provided an opportunity for analytical and in-depth probing into the effectiveness of many marketing activities – the annual budget – has remained a routine corporate exercise, with too much looking backwards at past allocations. Budget discussions have also suffered from the compartmentalized culture with a tendency to be department-focused – ie finance, production, sales/marketing – excluding any analysis of the customer value-chain. Accounts receivable continue to be handled by finance and design by research & development (R & D); their respective budgets and expenditure reviews are treated in the context of separate functions, headed by different managers whose concern is solely defending its own 'turf'.

The organizational budget timeframe, frequently mirroring the financial year, does not present the best conditions for a dynamic review of the overall marketing activity, with a longer-term vision of the diverse activities. The budget process degenerates into little more than number-crunching procedure, enacted at the same time each year to discuss and rubber-stamp major categories of overhead expenditure: many of the expenditures involving marketing activities escape a more thorough appraisal. At times of budget restrictions, and unlike decisions associated with capital investments of any size, marketing budget holders typically respond with a readjusted figure based on last year's appropriation and the forthcoming year's sales projections. This is accompanied by subjective judgements about what worked then and what might work in the next period.

Rule of thumb and incremental budgeting have characterized marketing budget-setting rather than a serious analysis of the programmes' payback, net present value (NPV) and internal rate of return (IRR). In spite of increasingly abundant information and data provided by technology, marketing has lacked sophisticated tools, especially when compared to other management functions like accounting. Quantifying the subjectivity that is inherent in many marketing decisions is no longer adequate, as the marketplace becomes more complex and competition intensifies across former national boundaries.

In short, the budgeting process associated with marketing remains an ossified mechanism with too much reverence for the past and too short-term in focus.

THE RISE OF MARKETING POWER

In retrospect, it is easy to see how marketing has arrived at this situation over the past two decades. Its ascendancy to power was driven by the spectacular prosperity in the developed economies following World War II. Riding on the wave of the renewed growth in practically every sector of the economy for basic consumer goods, many manufacturers found the 'marketing concept' an attractive model to adopt. The relentless pursuit of customer satisfaction became en vogue. With objectives set in terms of companies focusing, in a myriad of ways, on the satisfaction of customer needs, thereby winning their loyalty, most organizations in the 1950s were poised to dominate the packaged goods industries. This was enhanced by scale strategies matching the needs and market opportunities of the day. The emergence of a mass middle-class market with an insatiable thirst for consumer goods, imbued with relatively homogeneous tastes and life-style aspirations, provided an additional incentive to companies to boost volumes and standardize marketing activities.

Two other features significantly contributed in facilitating this trend: (1) retailing groups did not represent a powerful force in the marketplace and did not exert as much influence on the market as they command today; in any event, they lacked the management skills to exploit the situation; (2) mass TV advertising, penetrating every household, a massively popular news and entertainment medium that was to become the most powerful element in the marketing war chest.

The marketing policy employed by companies centred on getting the right 'marketing mix' balance, which was defined in terms of simple and controllable concepts of product, promotion, place and price – the infamous '4 Ps'. Among the techniques a company could employ were market segmentation, product differentiation and a mysterious blending of the elements of the marketing mix; clever manipulation of this mix, together with relatively low-cost TV advertisements, could guarantee the company a privileged relationship with consumers. Proliferation of products – and the building of brands – became the key plank of the marketing function, and the justification for its ever-growing budgets.

This winning formula was not destined to last forever, although it was seductively easy to believe that it would continue. By the early 1970s, marketing heads were having to respond to radically different sets of market forces. The comfortable market barriers that has so long protected companies were beginning to be dismantled. Across the globe, other socio-economic factors emerged to shake up the traditional approach.

- The increasing power exercised by the distribution/retail groups, as they moved across frontiers in search of customers and lower-cost sources of supply.
- The emergence of own-brands or distributor-brands launched by the retail trade at lower prices to appeal to a wider composition of the consuming population.
- The significant change in demographics in the developed world, led by the rapid ageing of the population, the shift of the baby-boomers into middle age and the falling fertility rates.
- The impact of information technology (IT) in reducing the time-to-market, lower but productive production runs and the introduction of new virtual communications vehicles to reach an increasingly dispersed and fragmented market.
- The contraction of product life-cycles and the emergence of

market saturation for basic consumer durables, on a world-wide scale.

THE MARKETING STRUCTURE

Organizational structures matching the growth and diversity of marketing activities and initiatives did not always keep pace with the rapidly changing environment outside the corporation. As a result, innovation and change were not particularly conspicuous features of many marketing departments. The need for marketing to be a company-wide philosophy – and not just an array of functional tools in the hands of a few – embracing a business process transcending multiple departments, has run into daunting complexities. Yet corporate advisers and management consultants frequently sounded the alarm bells by telling corporate heads that to respond to changing consumer preferences, competitive pressure and growing retail power in the marketplace, marketing decision-makers should constantly question its existing structures, strategies and tactics.

Faced, however, with the necessity to constantly adapt, marketing heads preferred to stick to a traditional set of marketing strategies and practices that have proven successful in past conditions. These become ossified into rigid attitudes and procedures handed down from one team to the next. Looking back over the post-war period, it is easy to see why this situation occurred and was actively sustained until the 1990s; it was inherently less risky to extend product lines and opt for variations of the same products for different market segments.

The ossified approach to marketing is anchored in the near-feudal structures of corporations of the 1950-70 period: marketing departments, frequently transformed and expanded from the original sales department, became large, divisionalized and functional entities, characterized by multiple hierarchical layers of management, functional expertise, integrated activities and hardened distinctions between line and staff people. The prevailing view held was that the larger the department, the more activities it could carry out by itself and thus obviating the need to contract out specific tasks to other firms. Size became blurred with the notion of efficiency through economies of scale.

Marketing heads, and the people staffing the function, evolved slowly in analysing all the available data and in considering the options aimed at maximizing profitability. But then again, the world up to the mid-1970s was moving at a slower pace, helped by convenient cross-market barriers to trade, and there were few real global players to disrupt this cautious and cosy approach.

A generation of marketing professionals saw their role defined in terms of gaining a thorough understanding of the market structures, the needs of the consumer and the appropriate sales technique to reach them at the optimum cost per 1,000 customers. This ensured that the massive capital investments made in production facilities were deployed in making goods that the consumer actually required. The trend towards centralization in the 1960s created the basis for marketing expertise in-house, and provided for economies of scale for the purchase of marketing services from outside 'experts' such as advertising and market research. Even when this structure gave way to decentralization in the late 1970s and throughout the 1980s, with its emphasis on making managers more responsible for their decisions, this was not always accompanied by enhanced marketing effectiveness.

The global marketplace of the 1980s and 1990s forced management to downsize and pursue acquisitions and mergers, many on an international scale, in order to build critical mass and survive; for some corporations, this proved to be over-ambitious, and there were shareholder concerns that massive investments were being poured into over-rated assets. In strict financial terms, only 28 per cent of cross-border mergers and acquisitions were successful. The reasons for failure were multiple: cultural misfit, a mismatch of technologies, market dissimilarities, and non-complementary distribution channels, etc. Foreign forays into acquisitions and mergers also tended to distract senior management's attention away from the key issues facing the company, such as the changing customer profile in their core markets.

With the shifting emphasis now on profits as a measure of corporate success and an economic slowdown and recession in the early 1980s and 1990s, marketing people are back to a more austere approach: stick to your knitting, focus on your core business and do what you do best. This has led to managers steering clear of diversification for its own sake, which has seemed prudent given the failures of the past. It has also led to a diminished level of ambition, preferring to streamline core businesses rather than push more assertively for higher sales.

An obsession with operational effectiveness has given birth to a concern that corporations may risk forgetting core aspects of what makes their business distinctive. Professor Michael Porter of the Harvard Business School predicted that the result could be a world of zero-sum competition in which productivity improvements cancel each other out, and companies benchmark and outsource themselves to the point where they all look alike.

Adding to the marketing function's woes is the criticism that companies had concentrated too much on product proliferation and differentiated marketing strategies, leading to highly diverse and costly marketing programmes. In recent years, policies based on multiple market segments backed by differentiated marketing (ie product variations and tactically different promotional campaigns) made the task of identifying cost factors considerably more difficult and stretched management resources. Each product could have variations, options and parameters to cater for specific national and regional markets. Concurrently, many customer groups were eligible for special treatment depending on their needs – ie differentiated packaging and usage instructions, frequent low-volume deliveries, specific in-store promotional support. All of this, of course, added up to customer satisfaction, but the economies of such strategies were not always fully examined and assessed from a cost/revenue relationship perspective.

By adding more product lines, the theory went, overheads could be reduced by spreading the costs thinner. This had the effect of making the figures look better but resulted in an accounting and overhead allocation structure that was difficult to manage. Companies ended up not knowing which product or segment was contributing to profit. Studies on 'costs-to-serve' different customer categories reveal that it is five time more costly to develop and retain new customers than retain existing ones. Yet, many consumer-product manufacturers persist in putting more effort into increasing the diversity and size of their markets, rather than sustaining activities amongst segments they have spent so much on developing.

Marketing experts, meanwhile, predict that advertising, the flagship of the marketing mix for many food companies, is losing power in the consumer products' market. Some of the reasons identified for this diminishing value are:

■ the growth of retailers' own-brands, cutting off manufacturers

from the consumers
- mass audiences are fragmenting, as a result of satellite TV and other media
- food manufacturers have wrongly focused on products and processes rather than their foods' essential qualities.

CHALLENGES FACING THE MARKETING STRUCTURE

While the debate about structure and focus of the marketing function prevails, larger forces in the environment initiated in the 1970s are still at work, many evolving in global magnitude. The European Single Market taking shape is but one factor, involving serious re-thinking about product features, uniform pricing, promotional tools and distribution structures. Companies have remained impotent in the face of these challenges; others have discovered that taking products and marketing tools across barrier-free frontiers has concentrated corporate minds on the need to respond.

In this book, the author attempts to highlight some of the central features in the marketplace that require a thorough re-assessment of traditional marketing policy. The basic assumption is based on the realization that consumers are no longer a homogeneous mass of people with similar tastes and buying habits; the world is demographically and socially a different place from that of the post-war period. Many of the marketing tools used in the past, such as mass advertising and branding, have been diluted by the arrival of cyberspace marketing, cheaper store-brands and time-obsessed working couples with less enthusiasm for traditional shopping. Marketing will have to find ways of identifying profitable market segments and deliver customer satisfaction in order to ensure renewed revenue streams in the future. This requires re-examining the '4 Ps' and their relevance *vis-`a-vis* its position in the market.

On the cost side, more attention has to be spent on identifying the real cost drivers in the business and figuring out the frequently indirect costs-to-serve for different market segments. The ensuing chapters will look at the challenges facing the marketing function, all of which have implications from a revenue and cost perspective. The magnitude of these challenges are briefly described below.

The fragmented customer base

Changes in consumer needs and perceptions have emerged, albeit somewhat more incrementally in Europe, as a result of social and behavioural transformations in society. Dual-earner households, more emphasis on leisure pursuits and increased levels of real income have all conspired in changing consumers' needs. Larger proportions of the female population are coming into the workforce – an estimated 83 per cent of all European women and 75 per cent of American women now hold some form of remunerated occupation. Additional income streams from this source have now become available for purchasing consumer goods not necessarily considered as necessities, such as second vacations, cars, bank accounts and credit cards. But it has also led to a rapid transformation in buying habits. With women combining paid employment and family responsibilities, the female no longer holds the sole role within the household for weekly shopping. Less time spent at home to handle the traditional chores means that the working female will seek out ready-made food products and time-saving devices.Within traditional family units, women continue to do most of the household tasks, but men now shop for an average of two and a half hours a week against four hours for women. Yet the bulk of brands are still targeted at women in the developed world.

Marketing has suffered from an over-reliance on standard perceptions of demographics, market research and mass-media advertising, resulting in misdirected strategies. Too much of marketing is still anchored in the demographic-focused strategies popularized in the 1950s, when companies concentrated primarily on marketing consumer necessities; today, much of consumer purchasing is discretionary. The reality is that markets are fragmenting as demographics reshape the composition of the population in favour of older customers with extended life expectations and a middle-aged baby-boomer bulge. In current and future conditions, there is growing evidence that market fragmentation will continue and even accelerate. In the USA, for example, major food companies are grasping the reality of a country that has as many as 100 distinct regions with clear local preferences. European white goods' manufacturers are also facing this problem in Europe, having discovered the stark reality of a less than homogeneous market with distinct regional preferences.

European food companies were able to exploit these conditions in the post-war years by invading each region's highly fragmented food markets with heavily promoted products like tinned fruit and baby foods. But growing affluence has re-created fragmentation: more money doesn't mean that it is spent on food. The changing shape of the European family of fewer children, more single households and an ageing population has resulted in families living differently, eating differently and eating at different times.

Demographic changes

Traditional markets are no longer occupied by people who fall into neat, clearly defined slots, categorized by A, B, C1 and C2 sociogroups. Nor is the presence of a 'unified' 370 million European Single Market a continuing justification for companies to believe that uniform needs for products and services exist on a grand scale. Demographics, more than the deadlines to meet the EMU criteria and the scramble to be ready for the euro, are evolving into the single most important influence on corporate strategies. The population of Europe grew by 63 million over the 1980s but will register an increase of only 10 million over the 1990s. The birth rate in the 15 EU states has dropped to 1.43 children per woman, its lowest since 1945, down from an average of 1.5 during the 1994-5 period; in Japan the births per woman have remained at an all-time low of 1.42 births in 1995 while 15 per cent of the population is aged 65 and over.

These trends have drawn a stream of dire predictions from economists and sociologists about dwindling consumption. In much of the Anglo-Saxon world, demographics no longer guarantee strong growth in home loans. The ageing of the population contributes more significantly to long-term financial products such as pensions. Building societies and banks have realized that they cannot grow rapidly without pursuing a strategy exposing them to wider financial services.

Meanwhile, the baby-boomer generation – the largest segment of the population – is ageing. In the 1980s, when baby-boomers were in their 30s, they went on a spending spree. Now in their 40s, they have most of the products they need to live a comfortable life-style. But they are far from being a uniformly prosperous and homogeneous group as previously thought; their expectations and perceptions have undergone a significant shift in purchasing emphasis, largely accelerated by the recession and downsizing. Their priorities have changed: they are spending their money on school fees for their children, retirement plans and nursing care for their parents. Retailers in the USA have been quick to note the changing spending habits amongst this important group and its contributing factor to weak consumer demand in the late 1990s.

Again, mass marketing in the face of demographic change is no longer sustainable; nor is the pursuit of over-extended, differentiated strategies for diverse demographic segments a solution.

The growth of retail power

The most noticeable impact on marketing has been the spectacular rise of the supermarket and hypermarket chains in practically every European state, to the detriment of the independent and co-operative grocery store. The grocery discounters' share has now dropped to below 10 per cent in the Netherlands, Spain, Finland, the UK, France and Italy; over the last five years the super/hyper groups have recorded annual sales growth of 6 per cent. Replaced by lower distribution overheads, groups like Carrefour in France, Sainsbury in the UK and Ahold in the Netherlands, have challenged manufacturers in search of price concessions and favourable payment terms. Armed with better cost savings ratios, the supermarket groups have passed on the savings to consumers in the form of lower prices. A proportion of these economies has also been used to build strong brand reputations by offering a wider choice of products and more innovative shopping environments. In many developed countries, such groups literally dictate the type of products they want, the pricing modalities and the delivery schedules.

Savings accrued from such muscular power are now being earmarked for enhanced IT spending to track the behaviour of consumers, thereby allowing them to develop a detailed picture of their consumers' needs to offer a better and more targeted service. Manufacturers now compete alongside the retailers to communicate with the consumer to build loyalty, in a more crowded marketplace. However, with government planning requirements tightening across the EU, the growth of discounters, the use of increasingly sophisticated technology and the rise of home shopping, the super/hyper groups are having to re-think future strategies – with their suppliers – to compete.

Widening price elasticity

Price competition in most industries is far more intense than in the pre-1970s period, brought about partly by the ever-growing consequences of deregulation and global competition. Technology has also enabled small-to-medium sized enterprises (SMEs) to enter markets previously well protected by larger and more established businesses.

Large brand manufacturers could always rely on the economies of scale policies of the past, which gave them a distinct advantage in sheer weight of product range and volume; it also allowed them a certain degree of discretion in setting pricing policy. IT developments have now provided the SMEs with the possibility to target specific market segments and niches, and compete alongside the giants.

Manufacturers of national brands now watch, with dismay, the dismantling of entry barriers in their traditional markets, the evidence of shortening product life-cycles and the perennial struggle to maintain market share. These changes have made it difficult for companies to raise prices – even in the face of rising costs.

Trimming costs and identifying added-value

One of the most important challenges facing corporations is the measurement of the costs of the 'knowledge' content of products and services, which continue to climb as a proportion of total costs relative to labour and materials. Economists now acknowledge that more value is added through design, styling, manufacturing-engineering, process-engineering, advertising and a whole range of ill-defined activities in the field of marketing. The concern has shifted to one of identifying those non-added-value activities which do not justify continuing resources, and either stripping them out or re-deploying the resources to more profitable customer-related tasks.

Clearly, being consumer-conscious is no longer enough if large parts of the organization still handles tasks that are provided at a disproportionate cost relative to the consumer's needs, or if whole customer categories contribute marginally to the bottom line. Pursuit of the concept of satisfying the consumer at any cost – or, worse, without knowledge of the real costs – can result in misdirection of resources and effort.

Such concerns cannot be taken lightly. Recent research suggests that (1) capital cost, R & D and marketing now represent 75 per cent of the total corporate costs in developed economies, and that (2) selling and general administrative costs are growing three times faster than materials or direct labour costs. Revelations of this magnitude make it vital to reconsider the real cost of sustaining business with different categories of customers, market segments and distributors. 'Blanket-bombing' advertising campaigns linked to undifferentiated mass-marketing techniques are not only singularly ill suited to today's marketplace, but are also wasteful. Equally, differentiated products combined with excessive market segmentation can lead to a small proportion of the overall customer base being truly profitable. Yet many companies continue to dissipate their increasingly limited resources over too many market segments and pursue a policy of product proliferation. Consumers, meanwhile, are either confused or express indignation at the vast array of choices or apparent lack of logic in producers' offerings.

Two important concerns arise here for marketing management's attention: first, corporate staff close to the marketplace know intuitively that unproductive time can be spent in the normal course of a day handling issues that are not related to anything that is happening on the sales floor or in the sales territory. This requires using their knowledge to guide a systematic and continuous search for processes, events, paperwork, sign-off procedures, internal rules, etc that simply distract staff from their key role in handling customers. Yet companies tend to be cautious in addressing this source of hidden cost, if only because the tasks fall within different responsibility centres making it difficult to resolve problems in a process-driven fashion.

Second, product lines and marketing distribution channels have proliferated in recent years in response to the greater market fragmentation. Common sense would suggest that the complexity of managing and servicing diverse market/product segments adds up to greater costs. The absence of appropriate costing systems to track and identify the comparative profitability of each, and the incremental costs associated with each, almost guarantees that product cost distortions will occur. Furthermore, direct labour now represents a declining proportion of total corporate costs, while costs generated by plant support operations, marketing, logistics and other overhead functions have grown three times faster.

Management accountants still allocate these growing overhead and support costs by their diminishing labour base; marketing and logistics costs are treated as period expenses and are not re-allocated at all. Attempts to apply the 'financial accounting' rules to these costs as being those charges below the gross margin line, reveals little in measuring the real product costs.

RESPONDING TO CHANGE

Some preliminary conclusions can be drawn from the vast changes that have taken place in the past two decades in guiding marketing heads to assess the entire marketing function and making it more responsive to changing conditions.

Redefinition of marketing

Marketing, as a function and discipline, must be responsible for more than the sale. It has to be redefined in terms of an all-embracing management function for ensuring that all aspects of corporate policy and its business is focused on delivering value-added service to the customer. Increasingly, it will not be able to do this alone. The 'stakeholder' approach will become more attractive in finding global solutions for an increasingly demanding customer base such as suppliers, distributors, technology providers, internal support services and the customers themselves. The whole organization must be implicated in this move. Marketing managers, who continue to see their essential purpose as selling whatever production happens to make, rather than working with stakeholders to design the product and service to suit the changing preferences of the customer, may not make it into the 21st century.

Abandonment of reliance on past experience

Reverence for past experience concerning what the consumer wants and how they can be reached is simply no longer a reliable guide to what is needed in today's globalized marketplace; it is even less relevant – and more dangerous as a signpost – for future activities. Market and social conditions have changed, new technology and competitors have emerged; the environment in which companies must now operate has changed so significantly and rapidly that marketing heads may not be monitoring and assimilating the right signals. Life-long learning and skills updating has a role to play here in contributing to improved decision-making.

The marketer of the 21st century must acquire a myriad of different skills, far broader than was expected of him or her in the past. Marketing guru Philip Kotler, in an address to an American Management Association conference in 1994, remarked that 'the skills to market via advertising management and salesforce are becoming less of the full value needed to build a brand loyalty'. At a time of major transition and deconstruction in marketing', he asserted, 'many of us will be obsolete'. The solution, many believe, lies in professionalizing marketing. An understanding of geo-demographics and customer-value analysis, together with a grounding in financial accounting will become an essential part of this new professional approach needed to assist the marketer navigate in a considerably more complex environment.

Analysis of the marketing effort

Analysis of the marketing effort must move beyond traditional revenues, costs and profitability to find the point at which marginal cost equates with marginal revenue to maximize profit. Deeper analysis, assisted by improved financial costing techniques, is required to determine if whole customer groups, distributors and market segments are worth pursuing on a sustainable basis. Marketing departments need to be responsible for more than their 'revenue centre' objectives. They should also possess the knowledge of the cost of sales and the proportionate costs of every aspect of the business that is focused on delivering value to customers. A lack of awareness of the full cost of servicing each market segment and managing the distribution channel is no longer sustainable at times of restricted resources.

Better cost information enables management to readjust pricing policy to respond to different categories of customers with different needs, or look for ways to reduce non-productive tasks that absorb internal resources. Building strategic partrillioner relationships with distributors will also be facilitated on the basis of more informed dialogue about costs linked to their business (low-volume deliveries, stringent payment terms, modifications to products, heavy customer support activities). Of central importance, is the necessity to have information to take the correct decisions relating to trade-offs between costs and revenues.

Intensified competition

Competition will intensify. The European Single Market has put an end to the days of safe domestic sales; competitors from Asia are ever-more aggressive; eastern European companies provide low-cost products of increasing quality. The answer lies in better target marketing, closer monitoring of all the costs associated with the customer life-cycle and greater innovation in product design, engineering, customer service and distribution.

Innovation and sustainable advantage

In times of intensfied competition and over-crowded markets, innovation also forms the basis of sustainable advantage when the company continually looks 'a customer ahead'. The current customer base may age, disaffect, or shift its buying behaviour – leaving behind obsolete products and inappropriate marketing tools. Looking a customer ahead is not an isolated and ephemeral task to be assigned to the advertising agency or business-school trainee; it is an integral and continuous part of management at all levels, in monitoring the social, demographic and geo-political shifts that could create new customer groups or uncover latent market opportunities. Peter Drucker describes this process by suggesting that companies can look a customer ahead by continually preparing itself for obsolescence. But this requires an 'all-hands-on-deck' corporate-wide approach to listening to the market and monitoring signs of change and opportunities.

Exploiting IT

Exploiting IT to solve customers' problems will become as important in adding value as the size, fixed assets, inventory and other tangible assets of the company. Again this requires a corporate-wide approach and not an isolated, departmentalized initiative. IT investments will produce results if focused on customers' concerns in four specific but inter-related ways.

- First, information needs to be captured on a common database and shared across the organization about customers, their buying habits, payments patterns, preferences, expectations, service requirements, etc. The 'islands of information' approach to capturing and exploiting customer-related data is simply no longer appropriate in today's competitive environment. Each staff member should have electronic access to this information and be able to contribute to the knowledge base. Up-to-date and relevant information will enable all functions to fine-tune their policies in harmony.

- Second, gaps must be filled in the electronic process through the Internet or e-mail to incorporate outside stakeholders such as suppliers of services and customers, thereby reducing excessive paperwork and onerous signing-off procedures and enhancing interactive problem-solving.

- Third, companies need to use IT to implement mass customization, ie collecting streams of information from various sources and allowing customers to access a customized version of the service.

- Lastly, senior management should insist on accelerating the pace towards a paperless environment, eliminating time-consuming tasks frequently done by multiple people in the same organization and encouraging less documentation associated with order-taking/processing and settlement practices.

KEY ISSUES

- An insulated and compartmentalized marketing function does not provide the best basis for servicing the customer; the diverse parts of the organization handling customer tasks – from design to accounts receivable – must function as an integrated whole in delivering customer satisfaction.

- If the company's marketing strategy and resources fail to satisfy the customers, greater efficiency through streamlining will minimize losses but this is rarely a substitute for increased revenue.

- Obsession with cost reduction, diversification and acquisitions can harm the relationship with current customers; senior management's vision and effort can be inordinately distracted from running the business and retaining the existing customers.

- The corporate budget process relies on too much reverence for the past and is too short-term-focused to be of meaningful use in providing a basis for in-depth appraisal of the longer-term implications of the marketing programme.
- A combination of changing demographics, highly competitive distributor own-brands, contracting product life-cycles and increasingly fragmented markets have conspired to make many of the traditional marketing approaches and tools redundant; mass-marketing aimed at homogeneous markets is obsolete.
- Companies do not add value by pursuing policies of product proliferation or by servicing increasingly diverse market segments; policies based on product customization in multiple market segments and backed by differentiated marketing may add up to customer satisfaction at local level, but may not be economically viable.
- The marketing function has to be responsible for more than the sale; customer satisfaction is an all-embracing management function, transcending functional departments throughout the organization, and focused on delivering an integrated value-added service. Disintegration of internal services leads to customer problems being stalled between functional barriers.
- The marketer of the future needs a broader range of skills and competencies than in the past: geo-demographics, customer-value analysis, financial accounting and an understanding of the costs associated with his or her business.

BIBLIOGRAPHY

AMA Forum Marketing, 'Creating a value-added strategy' (May 1997)

AMA Management Review, 'Master marketer' (interview with P Kotler) (April 1996)

M Batstone, 'Men on the supermarket shelf', *Financial Times* (2 October 1994)

A Benady, 'Difficult numbers to figure out', *Financial Times* (19 May 1997)

J Brady and I Davis, 'Marketing's mid-life crisis', *The McKinsey Quarterly*, 2 (1993)

N Conte, 'De la veille á écoute: le marketing se dévoile', *Le Figaro èconomie* (21November 1994)

D Dearlove, 'Who needs management?' *The Times* (London) (18 July 1996)

R Duboff and C Carter, 'Reengineering from the outside in', *AMA Management Review* (November 1995)

The Economist, 'Fat boys have fun' (29 April 1989)

The Economist, 'You ain't seen nothing yet' (1 October 1994)

B Ettore, 'Don't just think global marketing. Breathe it', *AMA Management Review* (September 1994)

F Glémet and R Mira, 'The brand leader's dilemma', *The McKinsey Quarterly*, 2 (1993)

Irish Marketing Journal, 'The collapse of mass marketing' (1996)

A Jeffries, 'Accountants urged to get a grip on marketing', *Management Accounting* (January 1995)

T Levitt, 'Marketing myopia', *Harvard Business Review* (July-August 1960)

T Levitt 'The globalization of markets', *Harvard Business Review* , no. 3, (May-June 1983)

P Loewe and D Hanssens, 'Taking the mystery out of marketing', *AMA Management Review* (August 1994)

A Martinez, 'Reebok: sprinting ahead through influence marketing', *AMA Management Review* (November 1988)

C Meeus, 'Le marketing nouveau est arrivè', *Le Figaro économie* (10 October 1994)

A Mitchell, 'Some like it hot', *Financial Times* (15 September 1994)

S Sommaruge 'La notion de service devient primordiale', Le Mois (Société de Banque Suisse) (October 1996)

J Spector/McKinsey & Co, 'Creative cost cuts needed', *South China Morning Post*, 27 (April 1990)

D Summers, 'Corporate zits beware', *Financial Times* (14 April 1994)

K Ward, 'Accounting for marketing', *Management Accounting* (May 1995)

F Webster, 'The changing role of marketing in the corporation', *Journal of Marketing*, 56 (October 1992)

2

MERGERS AND ACQUISITIONS - DO THEY ADD VALUE TO MARKETING?

Throughout the 1980s, the face of the corporate world was transformed by a storm of mergers and acquisitions (M & As); this trend was to continue, and even proliferate, over the 1990s. The fundamental difference between the two decades was the evolution of corporate thinking regarding M & As: whereas the 1980s takeover vogue was highly financially motivated and leveraged, the takeovers of the 1990s were more strategically-driven. What effect either motivation had on adding value to the marketing operation is harder to measure.

Much of the justification for this activity has been the desire to stretch corporate marketing power and managerial skills over different products and markets and across frontiers, thereby reducing the risks associated with the simpler but more vulnerable domestic product/market existence. Indeed, equity markets lavished praise on companies which were highly diversified and, *ipso facto*, capable of delivering higher income streams as their products and markets grew. From the marketing perspective, the M & A thrust had its attractions: senior management could siphon off cash from the more established parts of the corporation and redeploy it to develop activities with a higher risk exposure but with enhanced cash-generation potential; by acquiring other companies, it also enabled ambitious corporations to 'buy' market share in new markets, thus avoiding the costly learning curve associated with building a market presence. In addition, diversified products and markets somehow helped to insulate the corporation from volatile economic cycles, thereby allowing its diverse activities ride out a slump while the more profitable parts carried the group as a whole. In the run-up to the European Single Market, M & A activities also spearheaded the corporate marketing thrust aimed at building critical mass: the necessity to be a key player in each market across the European Union (EU) was an ambition that could be achieved only via takeovers of existing operations in each country.

The arrival of global capital markets in the 1990s attenuated the virtues of the first argument. Investors have become more sophisticated and want to decide where and when they put their speculative funds in stable cash-generating businesses, rather than leaving it to mercurial conglomerate heads. The second argument lost its appeal as economic and business cycles moderated in the early part of the 1990s. Corporate heads themselves also reached the belated conclusion that running differentiated businesses across multiple markets world-wide was not such an easy task: managing a chain of fast-food restaurants was not like making soft drinks or running an airline – it required specific skills. Management was less prepared to manage the divergent market conditions in each country, sometimes requiring investments in highly differentiated and expensive promotional programmes to maintain market share. For many corporations, this meant imposing financial controls and reporting systems, with resulting managerial burdens both at HQ and in the field.

M & A ACTIVITIES – A RETROSPECTIVE VIEW

After two decades of intensified M & A activity throughout the developed world, research now reveals that a disturbingly large number of acquisitions do not work. One study found that only 28 per cent of all M & A projects actually succeeded. Critics of M & A strategies assert that such activities may not be producing the synergies and cost savings claimed by many senior managers. Part of the reason is that, while such ambitions may be valid from an industry logic perspective, many are poorly executed. In the USA, the probability of a takeover actually succeeding is 50/50, and that figure is relevant for a coherent unified market like the USA. Further evidence emerges from a study by the Mercer Management Consulting group, revealing that 57 per cent of all large deals worth more than $500 million did not deliver returns above the industry average three years after completion. Although comparable figures do not exist for Europe, experts believe that the results are broadly similar. Increased use of English as the business language and the improved communications arising from IT infrastructures like the Intranet do not seem to have contributed to facilitating mergers and acquisitions in Europe.

Clearly, the price paid for the M & A entity and the strategic fit have long been considered as key factors in determining the success of such activities: many investment experts feel that corporations have over-paid for their acquisitions and it is a fact that unrelated M & A deals are inherently more difficult to integrate. Compounding these factors are the problems associated with cultural mismatch, turf wars and departmental jealousies, delayed implementation, bungled integration, protracted transition and the ultimate risk that such projects may end in disaster. One common factor, however, that stands out as being the single most important determinant in making M & As a success or failure is the quality of the *ex post facto* decisions taken once the deal has been cut. Many of these decisions relate to the marketing operation. Success depends not only on the quality of the post-M & A management effort in integrating the entities, but in ensuring that the marketing programme is coherent and adds value: does the current range of products make sense in a multi-market environment? Are there gaps in the product range? Is there potential for forging partnerships with distributors across markets? Have promotional synergies been exploited? Can advertising be standardized? While these questions are being debated, it is easy to forget that the customer still has to be served: lost business opportunities, confusing signals and diluted image arising from the loss of familiarity, are risks that are amplified during the transition period.

MAINTAINING MARKETING MOMENTUM

For the staff at all levels, M & A activities can often be a traumatic and stressful experience. In the run-up to the deal, the thrill of the chase tends to cloud the judgement of senior management, resulting not only in over-payment for the acquired business, but also in a failure to (1) keep the two companies functioning efficiently, (2) retain the morale and motivation of the staff, and (3) sustain customer loyalty. These three objectives are difficult to attain if staff read about their ominous future in the press and the attendant publicity refers to past mediocre performance of the target company. Job dissatisfaction and even dysfunctional staff behaviour are common. Left unattended, stress and uncertainty devours productivity; typically, the top marketing performers update their CVs and move on, only reducing further the possibility of ultimate success of the activity.

The greatest loss to the new company can be from the front-line staff, such as salespeople, who have built up relations with customers over the years and who are fully acquainted with their needs. Little consideration is given to the unanticipated loss of the 'institutional or corporate memory': the in-depth knowledge and skills acquired by longer-serving staff as to how the company built its markets and product ranges, the intricate and sometimes personalized nature of foreign client relationships, the nuances of these overseas markets, the networking arrangements and so on. While there is a need to constantly improve and even question the corporate *modus operandi*, changes to the way it does things on a grand scale, especially in relation to the customer, can be disruptive in the longer term and costly to reinstate. The loss of key marketing staff and defected customers can be difficult to replicate in the new structure. Obsessive concerns by management about the financial logic of the deal can diminish the benefits of a stronger marketing operation arising from new skills and fresh perspectives.

THE HUMAN FACTOR

Many of these problems can be addressed early in the M & A process – at the time of the negotiations between the two entities. Failure to take rapid action to inform and reassure managers, staff and customers in both entities will ultimately dilute the value of the deal. Once the companies have been legally integrated, a window of opportunity of 90 days exists to put in place appropriate financial controls, devise a detailed integration plan, resolve staff issues and ensure customer retention. Risks and opportunities need to be managed.

- With the integration of the target company imminent, any unnecessary delays will compound staff uncertainty. Office chat, wasteful and diversionary speculation replaces normal work patterns; the longer these last, the less attention the customers receive and the greater the risk of them defecting.

- Staff will be on high alert and more open to change than at perhaps any time in the company's history, in spite of the uncertainty and stress. This condition can be exploited by acting
  promptly to unfreeze energy and initiative by staff in the target
  company. Encouraging initiatives to add customer value by
  reducing quality defects, improving customer communications, streamlining the order-processing cycles, etc can release
  productive energy.

THE HIDDEN CHARACTERISTICS OF COMPANIES

Recognizing the culture of the target company and tackling its 'way
of doing things around here' behaviour, requires careful handling.
Identifying the cultural similarities and the differences between
both companies can become clearer from in-depth interviews,
focus groups and workshops involving staff from both entities.
Clearly, procedural manuals relating to staff rules and financial
management will provide some insight into the culture of the company, but equally important are the hidden components of the
organization in terms of behavioural patterns. Frequently referred
to as the 'organizational iceberg', this phenomenon represents the
attitudes, communication modes, group processes, personality,
motivation and conflict characteristics of the entity (see Figure
2.1). Many of these factors can be directly or indirectly related to
customer concerns. For instance, an informal group process
between engineers and salespeople can reveal a productive working relationship that has proven beneficial in the past in solving
customers' problems. Documented departmental policies and formal reporting relationships may provide little insight into such
arrangements.

For the integrated company, these informal systems, processes
and networks can be essential in building an even more powerful
entity, especially if related to factors that are perceived by customers as being important, such as the prompt response to customers' enquiries after the sale; ignored or misunderstood, they
can be highly destructive. M & A activities that lead to job cuts
and disruptive restructuring clearly damage the hidden structure
of the organization, resulting in 'disconnecting' behaviour by staff.
Although not visible from reading the P & L Statement or other
corporate records, this 'disconnecting' effect can and does harm

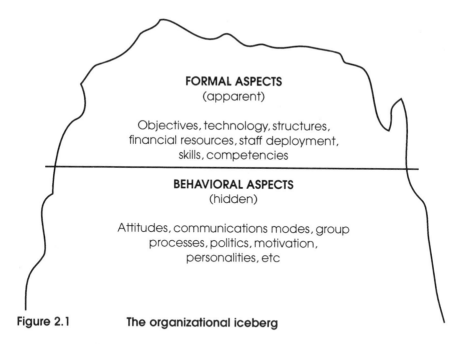

FORMAL ASPECTS
(apparent)

Objectives, technology, structures,
financial resources, staff deployment,
skills, competencies

BEHAVIORAL ASPECTS
(hidden)

Attitudes, communications modes, group
processes, politics, motivation,
personalities, etc

Figure 2.1   **The organizational iceberg**

customer relationships, if not recognized in time. Consider the example of the takeover of a regional soft-drinks' manufacturer in the US by a leading national food and drinks group, justified on the grounds that potential existed to add value by shaking up the *laissez-faire* way the regional company operated. Attempts to push the drinks through the acquirer's own distribution channels alienated staff, who preferred their more idiosyncratic ways of marketing the soft drinks. Profits quickly evaporated as both companies attempted to adjust, resulting in the bigger partner pulling out of the arrangement.

Understanding the culture of the new partner requires going beyond the visible signs of the formal processes. Any unilateral changes can impact on relationships with suppliers, distributors and, of course, customers. Consolidating synergies, based on years of close contacts with customers by sales staff, will depend on how the new formal systems interact with the company's culture and informal networks. If senior management ignores the staff's concern to value 'the way things are done around here' the M & A activity will run into resistance and the probability of failure will increase.

IMPLEMENTING CHANGE

Corporate cultures will, by definition, be fundamentally different, and it does not always make sense to force change. Aside from the difficulty in securing a consensus for change with the staff, there may be valid assumptions and procedures which are key to the proper functioning of the new entity. Ensuring a smooth transition should be a priority if there is a risk of customer defection. Avoiding conflict and keeping the customer happy requires building bridges between both companies.

■ Cultivate an atmosphere of learning (new procedures, sharing best models of marketing practice), which allows fresh assumptions to be fostered and implemented.

■ Make an effort to understand each other's culture. This can be facilitated through workshops, counselling and participative work groups of a cross-functional composition; the aim should be to articulate values, identify best practices and refine the mission statements.

■ Promote value continuity by seconding staff to the acquisition's business units to act as transition agents. They will also get an early opportunity to understand how the new partner or acquisition works.

■ Select the right people for the key functions in the new entity. This requires an equitable review of both internal and outside talent. Careful consideration must be given the relative advantages and disadvantages of choosing from either source. Although there are no hard and fast rules, senior management can minimize conflicts and increase their chances of selecting the right person by drawing up a list of options, as in Table 2.1.

Table 2.1 *Staffing the new entity: internal vs external sources*

Internal staff

Advantages	*Disadvantages*
Enhanced motivation of those selected	Narrow in-house perspective
Better assessment of abilities	Possible demotivation problems
Lower cost for some assignments	for those not promoted
Stimulates improved commitment and	'Political' infighting for
development performance	promotions
Triggers succession of promotions	Need for strong corporate
Entry-level recruitment only required	development programme

External staff

Advantages	*Disadvantages*
Brings new perspectives	Difficulty in finding or risk of not
Less costly than training an	appointing someone who 'fits'
internal candidate to a professional	May result in disenchantment for
level of competence	internal candidates
Absence of group of internal political	Longer 'adjustment' or period to
supporters	'come up to speed'
Opportunity to bring broader market	
sector insights	

DELIVERING THE BENEFITS

The implementation process is about delivering the benefits of the deal, and in particular, improvements to the marketing programme. A new organizational and reporting structure needs to be put in place, and a communications vehicle set up to explain the aims of the integration and of the new entity. But senior management also needs to act quickly to reduce conflict and keep the organizational momentum ticking over. This is particularly essential for functions dealing with the customer. Delayed deliveries, telephone calls that go unanswered and other manifestations of poor customer service lead to more lasting damage: disgruntled customers.

While successful M & A activities need strong leadership, senior figures associated with the deal cannot be everywhere at the same time. Steering committees and working groups referred to above can be useful in this respect, provided that they are (1) instituted early in the process, and (2) given clearly defined roles. These groups, comprising representatives from the two companies, can be formed either on a cross-functional or mono-functional basis. They provide a means of bridging the gaps between alliances formed in the separate entities and also in facilitating an overview of the global activity. Wasteful duplication and distorted communications throughout the organization can be avoided as a result. Senior management, thus freed-up, can assiduously keep an eye on customer-related activities, least they be forgotten in the process.

Formal communication of what is happening, throughout the M & A implementation process, cannot be stressed enough. Research shows the close link that exists between staff recognition that they were kept informed of developments and their belief that senior management took account of their feelings and valued their opinions. This helps to secure trust and confidence. Communications with staff should not lose the opportunity to emphasize the importance of keeping the customer happy. Given that M & A activities affect the whole organization, it is easy to neglect the continuing delivery of a range of services provided by different departments to the customer.

Once the deal is signed, no time should be lost in addressing these management issues in ways that strongly and visibly support the new entity – staff changes, redefinition of missions, redeployment of responsibilities and performance plans. The acquirer's obsession with the deal itself can easily overlook the steps involved in the complex affair of blending the different IT systems, informal processes and cultures that make M & A activities work. The danger is that managers of cost, revenue and profit centres are rarely involved in the M & A discussions but are the very ones who have to implement the post-deal integration strategy. Much of the value destruction linked to M & As actually takes place outside the responsibility areas of the managers who are directly concerned by these changes. Key decisions need to be taken about where the central functions like legal affairs, purchasing, personnel and finance should be located. It seems illogical to retain a duplicate copy of each function in the new entity; centralization of these functions will almost always be a necessity, and plans have to be devised to deal with surplus 'professional' staff.

Bringing together formal systems and processes without the opinion of the managers running these services can be fatal: the 'merger' of computer systems associated with the link-up between

two leading US banking groups proved so difficult that each set-
tled for a division of labour: one IT unit handled cheque processing and the other consumer banking; the ensuing chaos took 18
months to sort out.

MULTICULTURAL CONSIDERATIONS

Cross-frontier M & A activities create another set of complexities.
Dissimilar geography, culture and accounting systems add to the
sense that senior management cannot always move swiftly and
decisively. Acquisitions tend to be easier to implement compared
to mergers because one side is supposedly more in control of the
situation. But in the head count to make sure that representation
is equitable, the new entity does not always end up with the best
people. While, ultimately, such issues sort themselves out, anything from nine months to two years is absorbed in reaching the
optimum equilibrium. Again, in the transition period while these
problems are being worked out, senior management energies can
can be easily diverted. The 'top line' – the revenue-generating
activities – need equal attention during the M & A process. There
is a limit to cost savings that the M & A deal can deliver. Declining
sales arising from neglected customers cannot continue to be
compensated by further expense reduction.

LOCAL VS EXPATRIATE MANAGER

A global corporation built on progressive M & A activities presents
a particular challenge when it comes to selecting the right person
to run the new entities. Inevitably, the question arises as to the
suitability, and appropriateness, of a locally hired versus an expatriate manager. Two schools of thought dominate the debate in
many companies: should a policy be pursued to develop truly
internationally experienced managers or employ local managers
imbued with the culture of the organization? The optimum solution lies in finding a balance between both. Creating a cadre of
international executives in an increasingly global business environment makes a lot of sense. But a large proportion of the big
companies still has a culture rooted in their country of origin. This
results in overseas experience not being as appreciated; new skills

and local knowledge tend not to be exploited when the manager returns to HQ. While the rotation of key marketing staff may be desirable, the HQ perceive those who remain as expatriate managers of the new acquisition as 'cut flowers': they absorb new skills, languages and processes but lose them just as quickly and end up competing with the local managers. Then there is always the risk that the expatriate will not adapt. Anecdotal evidence shows how difficult it can be for expatriates to function in a foreign-acquired firm. These difficulties can arise from:

- the differences in the norms of behaviour between the expatriate manager's home country and those of the host country, and
- anxiety resulting from a sudden loss of familiar surroundings, especially for the family.

Even if the appointment of expatriates is fraught with multiple problems, sometimes resulting in the assignment being ended prematurely because of difficulties encountered by the manager (and the family) in adapting, companies with extensive global M & A activities may find equally compelling reasons for sending expatriates to head up the new operations.

- Staffing concerns locally – local managers may not fulfil the requirements of the job, both from an experience and qualifications perspective.
- Management development – the holding company may wish to provide younger 'star' category of staff with the opportunity to experience new challenges, develop new skills and run their own operations away from HQ; this could be important in retaining high-calibre staff.
- Organizational development – the organization as a whole may find it beneficial to cultivate a more 'rounded manager', experienced in different cultural and business environments, and to develop adaptability and flexibility; it also facilitates the creation of international contacts and networks.

Strategic or corporate policy concerns sometimes leave the organization with no alternative – in the short-term – but to appoint an expatriate manager to head up the local company:

- the company has no one sufficiently familiar with the foreign government to interpret communications, and feels it is necessary to develop an 'area' of cultural expertise

- virtually no autonomy is possible for the foreign arm as it is integrated so closely with operations elsewhere
- senior management is concerned about protecting high-tech knowledge and skills that are not easily safeguarded legally in some parts of the world
- the host country is multiracial or multireligious – and it is difficult to find a local manager not belonging to one of the conflicting races
- there is a compelling marketing need for the company to maintain a foreign image associated with the product or service
- locally hired staff are neither mobile nor interested in foreign assignments.

Finding the 'right' person to manage the new foreign merged or acquired company requires serious thought by the candidate and senior management to ensure that all parties have weighed up the pros and cons. A lucid analysis of the foreign assignment would include examining the factors outlined in Table 2.2.

Table 2.2 *Weighing up an expatriation assignment*

Benefits	Downside
Enhanced chance for responsibility	Dual-career families:
Chance of adventure and travel	difficult to 're-locate' partners'
Opportunity for fast-track promotion	skills
Reduced competition from peers	Partners reluctance to re-locate
Improved personal life-style and	outside country of origin
satisfaction	Risk of missing out on career
Broader experience	opportunity and networking in
Higher income	country of origin
	Continuity in children's
	education

Many corporate observers feel that the expatriate is an outdated legacy of the multinational days, when managers were dispatched from HQ like colonial administrators to run overseas possessions. Many corporations have shifted their hiring practices to employ locally hired managers in response to a combination of cost, legal and cultural factors. Some of the more pertinent reasons for hiring local managers are that:

- they are less expensive compared to expatriates
- they can facilitate cultural understanding between the holding concern and the local company
- labour law in some countries often requires that nationals be hired to fulfil certain tasks, such as accounting and auditing.

Increased efforts to trim costs – and, more importantly, exploit cost savings as a result of M & A activities – has put the spotlight on the high costs of sustaining expatriate assignments. Price Waterhouse, the international accountancy and auditing group, estimates that the average cost of expatriate assignments is $139,208, based on 1997 figures. This includes relocation, expatriation allowances, housing, extra tax and social security provision.

An increasingly noticeable trend is the reluctance of middle-aged managers with working spouses or partners and children to accept an overseas assignment. The potential danger of premature re-deployment of the manager back to HQ if the assignment doesn't work out, is also costly, not to mention the damage to the company's reputation *vis-à-vis* the distribution partners.

EMPOWERING THE LOCAL MANAGER

Pursuing a policy of hiring only local managers is not without its problems, however. If the senior management team at HQ is composed of only natives of the country of origin, difficulties will occur in retaining a high-calibre, global pool of managers. Foreign managers of new M & A entities may feel that they do not 'fit' with this type of operation. Retaining high-calibre local staff in organizations characterized by highly centralized management structures and a desire to standardize marketing policies can be a real challenge. When HQ takes decisions associated with new product development and sourcing, the initiatives left to local managers are likely to be limited and stifle innovation or creativity. Integrating and maximizing the skills of local managers requires a corporate-wide policy aimed at marshalling local and regional synergies and talent.

- Encourage local managers to contribute in developing new products, identifying market segments, reducing non-value-added activities and – more importantly – give recognition for these initiatives.

■ Incorporate senior local managers in the development of global and local strategic decisions on a rotating basis, so that each manager has had exposure to HQ planning exercises.

■ Devolve budget authority to local managers within broad spending limits in order to respond to local conditions and provide the basis for balancing trade-offs between costs and revenue decisions.

■ Designate different national companies as the 'lead countries' responsible for different activities such as after-sales service, billing, logistics, customer order-booking, etc.

As companies acquire and merge entities across the globe, reporting relationships with regional managers in a highly multicultural organization could become contentious. Even if the distances are not great – as in the European region – their integration and interaction with the HQ is vital. Empowering regional managers of different cultures is not achieved solely by e-mail and telephone communications. Nor should the dialogue be restricted to local issues in their region; the managers heading up the newly established corporate operations in each region should be considered as an integral part of the corporate team and the reporting and planning structures should reflect this dimension. They can be made to feel part of the corporate whole.

■ Solicit their views on corporate-wide issues – ie central services, opening new markets, product development and extensions, diversification, senior management appointments, etc.

■ Plan their visits to HQ at least four times a year to interact on issues of mutual interest; regular interaction of this nature with HQ staff helps to reduce uncertainty and cultivate networking on a wider scale.

Whatever the outcome of corporate policy with regard to expatriate vs local-hired managers, achieving fast integration and delivering value as a result of synergies arising from M & As requires a balance to be struck between:

■ locally-hired managers running the foreign operations to provide local knowledge, expertise and cultural links

■ a pool of internationally experienced managers capable of enriching the strategic thinking of the company and working with different cultures.

MANAGEMENT CONTROL – A SOURCE OF DISPUTE

The final aspect to be considered in any M & A activity is the management control dimension of the new entity – who has responsibility for what? The list of control factors can be long and contentious, depending on the complexity and international composition of the deal. Failure of M & A projects as a result of ill-defined management controls is legendary. Fiat's three attempts over the past 30 years to ally with another carmaker have foundered on the question of management control. A control policy is essential prior to the integration of various entities if potential conflict is to be avoided. Certain core issues need to be reviewed by all sides; Table 2.3 outlines a possible list.

Table 2.3 *Control factors: possible areas of potential conflict*

Ownership:	sale or transfer of equity to new parties, separation or consolidation of brands
Borrowing:	acceptable debt/equity ratios
Plant extension:	what and where
R & D:	level, purpose and location
Production processes:	degree of integration, degree of capital-labour intensity
Sources of supply:	external or internal, transfer prices
Quality standards:	domestic or absolute, international standards
Product mix:	diversification, competitive exports
Terms of sales:	credits, servicing, pricing
Market area:	restricted or open, separate or combined dealerships
Market penetration:	choice of channels, promotional effort
Staff-management relations:	worker participation or co-determination, negotiation culture
Management selection and remuneration:	nationality, skills required, decision-making style
Politics:	corporate governance policy, company- government relations, etc.

Even in the post-merger or acquisition phase, ongoing dialogue will still be necessary as the newly structured entity evolves and the external environment throws up new challenges. Ongoing review should include the following.

- Ownership – control over elections of Boards, development and redeployment of senior managers, determination of financial structure and profit distribution, corporate governance rules.
- Market access – control over distribution channels, trademarks, brand names and cross-frontier marketing policy on 'own-branding', etc.
- Resources and revenues – openness to the pooling of resources when innovations are exchanged with peer companies, agreeing on dividing common costs and revenues.
- Finance – ability to provide working capital and/or low-cost debt and equity.
- Staffing – ability to provide scarce skills at reasonable cost, including management input.
- Supply of components and finished products – limitations on sources for associated firms in the group, and the basis of transfer pricing.
- Marketing strategy – standardized approach (same product and communications strategy) or a more localized one (products and communications' strategies tailored to each market).

As an organization grows and becomes more geographically dispersed, the control function must evolve; otherwise, operations will tend to dissipate, with the resulting loss of opportunities, increased costs and, ultimately, a dissatisfied customer.

FINANCIAL CONTROLS

Control mechanisms are influenced by such factors as distance and location. As physical distances expand resulting from growing cross-frontier M & A activities, centralized HQ controls over the diverse operational entities may be necessary. One international hotel group, built up incrementally over time through acquisitions in each country, found that lack of central controls at HQ resulted in catastrophic financial performance. Under a scheme designed to devolve cost and revenue responsibilities to each hotel property, each manager could keep excess profits after paying an agreed rental to central HQ. Soon the individual hotels began to compete with each other for the same business and competition for custom from fellow group hotels forced the room rates down. Local managers, struggling with declining room rates and falling occupancies, found themselves constrained in generating revenue, while HQ continued to demand rental. The devolved system soon concealed the real problems at local level: since managers had to pay HQ in advance they never defaulted but suppliers, maintenance fees and other charges were either paid late or left unpaid.

Problems of this nature can be detected with appropriate central HQ-driven controls, and symptoms are apparent when:

- conflicts emerge between divisional or affiliate units over clients or sales territories in different markets
- poor or inadequate internal controls employed by foreign entities are revealed by auditors during a statutory audit exercise
- HQ administrative, human resources and finance functions duplicate those in place within foreign entities
- customer complaints relating to service-delivery and after-sales service start to grow in intensity and magnitude
- conflicts emerge between overlapping distributors in foreign markets or in national markets having the same affinities, ie language
- sales branches in the field show an increasing tendency to proliferate.

SHOULD MARKETING OPERATIONS BE DEVOLVED?

Subsidiary managers of global companies see marketing as being the biggest area of conflict between themselves and HQ, according to a Conference Board Europe study: the tendency is for HQ to continue to want to provide guidelines for marketing practice to be applied by all subsidiaries. Tight integration of policies relating to marketing has led to negative experiences, with local managers retaining profit responsibility but with little marketing decision-making power left in their hands to take local initiatives. The study suggests that local managers of global companies are losing more autonomy compared to expatriate managers – and this may not always be the best way forward when related to marketing decisions – expatriates have a tendency to implement strategy at a local level too rigidly.

Some of these problems can be overcome by striking a balance between the benefits of integration and centralized centres of excellence, regardless of where these are based in the world. This would consist of reducing the local manager's decision-making authority in each country over R & D, purchasing and manufacturing, these functions being consolidated in centres of excellence which may be centralized on a regional or global basis. Responsibility for marketing, meanwhile, would be shifted to the regional companies of the group under the responsibility of the local manager. Even under these arrangements, there is nothing to prevent the global company from encouraging a policy of sharing and transferring relevant marketing knowledge from one country to another.

Even within this revised marketing structure, there may be compelling justifications for integrating and centralizing certain tasks such as billing and collecting payments from one central geographic location, preferably in areas where there are proven indigenous skills available on a cost-efficient basis. In any event, a common agreement has to be reached on standardizing each stage of the 'market-to-collection' phase for all companies in the group, in order to (1) generate savings in staff and processing-time, (2) provide a benchmark for performance based on the region with the best-practice record, (3) enable the company to offer a consistent service to customers across multiple markets, while allowing for the inevitable variations caused by local law and custom. One copier and printer manufacturer with world-wide operations, for instance, discovered that substantial benefits arose from eliminating the time lost by sales managers chasing information that the company already held somewhere in its structure: up to 30 per cent of their time was absorbed in this task in each market. New integrated data-base systems accessible on a cross-border scale were devised to provide this information and help them to do a better job in the marketplace.

AVOIDING HEAVY HQ BURDENS

In a quest to achieve economies of scale, many corporations impose at the same time heavy costs on its local managers. Even if HQ has little knowledge of the local market conditions and tactics needed to win customers, it imposes its policies regardless. The danger arises where local managers spend more time trying to please head office than satisfying the customer. The 'internal customer' phenomenon, in time, becomes a misdirected effort by local managers, focused on meeting deadlines for submission of reports to HQ rather than on improving the local firm's capacity to generate sales or sustain customer satisfaction. Although internal reports, statistical analyses and meetings with HQ staff are important, such activities are more meaningful if they linked to a focus on the external customer – ie are the customer's problems being solved? If the local firm's role *vis-à-vis* the customer becomes more tenuous and increased reporting prerogatives contribute little to customer satisfaction, a serious reappraisal of the HQ/local firm's relationship needs to be considered.

M & AS – AN OPPORTUNITY TO IMPROVE MARKETING

Even where mergers and acquisitions make strategic sense, companies do not exploit the opportunity to (1) learn from best marketing practices in the other companies, (2) streamline and standardize marketing processes and practices and (3) generally revamp and improve the marketing thrust. The integration process following an M & A could be a catalyst to drive a review of the marketing operation. Three immediate concerns could be addressed.

Consistency in quality of services

One of the most complex issues arising from M & A activities is the presentation of a consistent image and maintaining customer service after the deal is struck. Key to this must be the emphasis on quality and improving standards. This does not mean blaming the staff for past failures but stressing on them the additional cost to the customer if work has to be corrected after delivery, because of mislabelled deliveries, incorrect keying in of customer orders, poor quality control, etc. The cost of doing things wrong amounts to 'failure costs' arising from poor attention to detail or inordinate paperwork associated with the customer value-cycle.

Articulating the benefits of the M & A decision

The second imperative is explaining to customers – frequently across multiple national markets – the benefits of mergers or acquisitions. This can be a long and costly task. An additional danger is that the revised marketing programme may simply result in the demise of the weaker brand or smaller partner. The new entity has to move quickly to spell out the benefits to the customer, such as convenience or improved quality of service, as a result of the merger. Inherent in this approach is the necessity to reassure customers that they will not lose the familiar when a merger results in a new identity. This was achieved by a US banking group following its merger with a similar financial services operation. It maintained brand equity by marketing three different types of funds, reflecting the investments for which each of the previous two banks were best known, and kept their previous brand names; the less well known and least well performing funds were dropped.

This point is driven home by many of the leading whiskey and beer brands, now forming part of integrated international groups with increased market power. For customers buying their favourite brand at the supermarket, the effects of consolidation were almost unnoticeable. Indeed, it made little difference who owned the brand, provided the image remained consistent. For others, the new owners became so preoccupied with acquisitions and sales of companies that they never got around to rationalizing the product ranges and consolidating the image of the remaining brands.

Adding-value services

The M & A activity can also be an opportunity to offer unique and added-value services to the customer. Merged electricity and gas utility companies in the USA have used their clout to become total energy suppliers, offering their residential, commercial and industrial customers the optimum solution to their energy needs. The aim is to offer 20-30 enhanced services, generating high profit margins in areas like home security, appliances repair and air conditioning services. Some marketing experts see this as encompassing links with telecommunications companies and cable TV operators to offer an even broader range of value-added services, such as time diagnostics that would alert the customer if the central heating was absorbing unanticipated wasteful energy in the house because of a fault in the system or poor insulation. Such alliances should also yield savings for the utilities by enabling companies to send out a bill to the customer for a range of utility services.

WHAT ARE THE ALTERNATIVES TO M & A?

In the international pharmaceutical industry, characterized by expiring patent protection, many companies have sought rationalization via the M & A route. The origin of the problem has been that older drugs that generated much of the growth in the past 15 years are losing patent protection and new drugs are being developed at too slow a pace to maintain future earnings. M & As have not proven to be beneficial in all cases. According to research carried out by AT Kearney, the US management consultants, M & A initiatives in this sector worth $100bn-plus in the past decade 'have generally had lower economic returns' than those which pursued other avenues for growth. 'Economic returns' are defined in the study as being equal to economic earnings (net operating profit less cost of capital), divided by economic value (total assets less non-operating assets, capitalized value of R & D and other elements), multiplied by 100.

AT Kearney point to a number of factors that have contributed to better performance amongst those pharmaceutical companies who have chosen an alternative route by going back to the basics of marketing:

- concentrating on a small number of medical areas – ie asthma, or digestive system drugs
- adopting the ability to learn from the marketing strategies and practices of the best consumer goods corporations – ie a therapy treatment sold directly to patents rather than via doctors
- willingness to outsource some services – ie partnerships formed with smaller R & D firms to carry out basic research
- taking on board the best practices in R & D of other companies – ie computerizing the regulatory work.

Two features characterize this approach, First, the recognition that over-extension of products in too many markets is increasingly difficult to manage. Companies do not build sustainable relationships with the customer and the distribution trade by swamping them with products; marketing effort is dissipated and customers end up with a confused image of the expertise that the company is really trying to establish in the marketplace. Second, useful and profitable insights can accrue from learning about how other successful companies approach marketing. Practices, procedures, communications modes and innovative distribution tactics can be adopted, albeit modified to take account of local market conditions.

STICK TO THE BASICS

As the 1990s' acquisition and merger boom reaches new heights, a distinctly worrying feature is the obsession with size that such activities provokes. Clearly, not every corporation can be the biggest, leading to M & A pursuits feeding on itself. Companies left behind in the rush to gain even greater economies of scale and marketing predominance are enticed to forge deals with each other to catch up. But in the exuberance to acquire and merge, senior management may lose sight of the value of these deals from the customer perspective. The statistic cited earlier in this chapter about mergers failing to live up to expectations – 57 per cent of M & A activities worth more than $500mn resulted in poor returns for shareholders in the ensuing three years – is far from theoretical. Analysts point to two fundamental reasons for this.

- First, companies fail to execute the deals, bearing in mind that the ultimate aim is not just shareholder value but increased levels of profitable customers. While management may be apt at quantifying the 'hard' costs of integration like layoffs, they possess less talent in measuring how disruptive the process can be. In this category one finds inhibiting cultural clashes between the two or more corporations, or precipitative cost-cutting measures which result in diminished customer service and inevitable customer disaffection. In the end, the bigger group is almost bound to become more bureaucratic in style, thus stifling initiative throughout the whole organization.
- Second, M & A-prone corporations fail to anticipate competitors' responses, such as an aggressive promotional reaction by

a rival or their ability to also match cost cutting via mergers. Cost synergies as a primary *raison d'etre* for mergers or acquisitions should not be the ultimate value of such activities.

KEY ISSUES

■ Research shows that 57 per cent of M & A activities worth more than $500mn resulted in poor returns for shareholders in the ensuing three years. Even when deals are more closely linked to the company's core strategy, only 50 per cent have a chance of succeeding.

■ Multiple factors affect the success of M & As; one of the most important ingredients is the quality of post-M & A management in integrating the entities and ensuring that the consolidated activities make strategic marketing sense.

■ Pre-and post-M & A phases require management attention to ensure a smooth transition, focused on ensuring that:

– high-calibre staff do not defect and take their 'institutional skills' with them
– inactiveness does not lead to drop in productivity and dysfunctionalism in both entities
– the transition and integration takes place promptly
– the customer needs and ongoing business contacts are not forgotten.

■ Disruptive restructuring and dispensing with organizational arrangements on a wide scale can be harmful to customer relations; understand the target company's culture and its relationships with distributors and customers.

■ Build value continuity by encouraging cross-mobility in each other's company to identify best marketing practices and eliminate unnecessary duplication and non-value-added tasks.

■ Multicultural M & As are more complex, requiring more time spent on sorting out the optimum structures, staffing arrangements and reporting systems.

■ With multiple geographical sites, review the pros and cons of expatriate vs locally hired managers to run the operations; both options can be expensive if the wrong people are chosen.

■ Find the optimum balance between developing a mobile cadre of internationally minded executives and motivated local managers capable of contributing to the strategic direction of the global company, and fostering an understanding of different cultures.

■ Identify, early in the process, any areas of management control where potential conflict between the entities could erupt – ie product mix, market territories, cross-market selling, choice of distribution channels, etc.

■ HQ imposition of marketing policy at a local level can be counter-productive; find the optimum balance between (1) the benefits of integrating marketing activities and (2) the value of centralized centres of excellence, at local or global level.

■ Consider common agreements with the different entities on standardizing each stage of the market to collection phase – ie billing, accounts receivable, customer servicing, etc.

■ Minimize inflicting HQ administrative burdens on the local entities to avoid the 'internal customer' phenomenon; it misdirects efforts away from sustaining customer's business in each market.

■ Identify opportunities arising from M & As for improving the marketing operations – ie added-value services to the customer, presentation of a consistent image and positioning, etc.

BIBLIOGRAPHY

C Adams, 'Safety at a premium', *Financial Times* (18 December 1997)

Anglo-German Foundation, 'Corporate restructuring in Britain and Germany', report (1997)

A Brummer and I King, 'Big business just got bigger', *The Guardian* (14 October 1997)

Certified Accountant (ACCA), 'Most acquired businesses perform poorly, says study' (March 1997)

Conference Board Europe, 'The changing global role of foreign subsidiary managers', report (1997)

L Copeland and L Griggs, 'Getting the best from foreign employees', *AMA Management Review* (June 1986)

R Donkin, 'The expatriate experience', *Financial Times* (14 November 1997)

The Economist, 'Why too many mergers miss the mark' (4 January 1997)

The Economist, 'Cut and paste' (1 February 1997)

Ernst & Young, 'Acquisitions and mergers: an introduction to buying and selling private companies'

Eurostat, 'Mergers and acquisitions in Europe' – Monthly Panorama of European Industry (1997)

P Festa and J Pannell, 'Merging people successfully', *Acquisitions Monthly* (June 1997)

D Green, 'Drug makers need new prescription for success', *Financial Times* (5 January 1997)

T Jackson, 'Time's up for the man from head office', *Financial Times* (8 October 1997)

J Kay, 'Learning to define the core business', *Financial Times* (1 December 1995)

W Lewis, 'Return of the mega-deal', *Financial Times* (10 October 1997)

R Mills, 'Shareholder value analysis in acquisition and divestment decisions by large UK companies', *Management Accounting* (February 1998)

D Nissan, 'A regional slice of the global pie', *Financial Times* (14 August 1995)

M Porter, 'The state of strategic thinking', *The Economist* (23 May 1987)

A Smith, 'A life after re-branding', *Financial Times* (10 February 1997)

K Smith and S Herschman, 'Making mergers work for profitable growth: the importance of pre-deal planning about post-deal management', Mercer Management Consulting (1997)

S Wagstyl, 'Arranged marriages', *Financial Times* (14 October 1997)

S Wagstyl, 'When even a rival can be a best friend' (22 October 1997)

3

DEMOGRAPHIC CHANGES AND MARKETING

While corporations world-wide dwell on the merits of extending their product lines and launching new brands, thereby creating what many marketing observers view as being excessive segmentation and consumer confusion, the core marketing issue fails to be addressed: defining the profile of, and appealing to, the transforming customer base. In a world of changing demographics, such considerations as brand extension policy and what marketing tools to be employed pale into insignificance on closer analysis of the increased fragmentation of traditional markets around the world.

Over-reliance on ossified demographic perceptions, redundant market research and sub-optimal mass media advertising focused on primary marketing necessities has become misdirected. The mass-marketing thrust of treating markets as homogeneous groups of people with standard tastes and aspirations has no place in contemporary marketing. Traditional markets throughout the developed world are longer occupied by clearly defined consumer segments, categorized by A, B, C1 and C2 socio-economic groupings. Segregation of consumers along these lines, accompanied by distinct marketing campaigns, used for the first 80 years of the Consumer Age, are singularly ill-suited to current – and future – conditions. Demographic changes have simply transformed the marketplace beyond recognition in the past two decades, creating for the marketing function a cocktail of new opportunities and threats:

■ ageing population structures and sharp declines in fertility rates in most countries of the developed world
■ baby-boomers moving into middle age
■ different values and life-styles of the emerging post-baby-boomers
■ the increasing participation of the female in the workforce

■ the more diverse cultural composition of the population.

What are the motives of these different demographic groups? What are the implications for marketers? This chapter attempts to describe the dramatic changes taking place, based on document-ed research and forecasts by various institutions. More impor-tantly, what are the marketing policy implications that arise from these changes?

THE AGEING POPULATION

For many years concerns have been raised by politicians about the key demographic shift taking place on a global scale: popula-tions almost everywhere are getting older faster. The focus of the debate has been the concern that if the level of state pensions is to be maintained as the number of eligible recipients grows, future work entrants, all things being equal, will pay higher taxes. This could signal diminishing real incomes and consumption expecta-tions for the emerging generations. But for the marketing world, the ageing population could represent an opportunity if the signs are detected in time and the corporate offerings adapted.

A population becoming older in the next decade hides a com-plex web of demographic changes, which will inexorably affect marketing policy. The consequences for how companies create, produce, market and sell their products will constitute a challenge that goes beyond a simple transformation from youth to older markets. The change in the age structure has significant implica-tions with regard to market structure and buying habits. Each age group has typical and varying habits so that the size of these groups can play a decisive role. The inter-relationship of these groups will, however, also change and thereby have an impact on the buying habits of these groups. The most striking example is in the USA, where the ageing process has led to predictions by Kenneth Dychtwald, a leading US social scientist, that the propor-tion of people over 55 will grow by 20 per cent by 2007, while those aged between 18 and 34 will drop by 3 per cent. This will be accompanied by a fundamental shift in US spending patterns: between 1946 and 1964, 76 million young people were entering the market place, provoking a demand for houses, credit cards and consumer goods aimed at the youth market. Changing demographics now suggest a scenario in which the spending behaviour of the 45-54 group will rise by 36 per cent and those under 35 will drop by 12.5 per cent. Successful marketing programmes to reach specific age groups now signifies a thorough familiarity of the habits of these groups, and early adaptation of products and communication tools to respond to changed circumstances. The fastest ageing segment of the market everywhere – those over 60 years – may hold the key to hidden potential.

THE FACTS...

In 1990, 500 million people world-wide were aged 60 or above, about 9 per cent of the global population. Predictions by the World Bank put this figure at 1.5 billion by 2030, or 16 per cent of the population. These trends are already reality in the OECD countries: more than 17 per cent of the population were aged over 60 years in 1990. The over-65s, for instance, currently represent on average 13.4 per cent of the EU population, the highest proportion of people over 65 living in the UK (15.1 per cent), with Germany and Sweden catching up with just under 15 per cent of the population in this age group. Nearly 15 per cent of the 125.7 million population in Japan is aged over 65, with OECD projections for the year 2025 placing Japan's elderly population ahead of every other industrialized country. The bottom line, in demographic terms, is that by the year 2000 some 18 per cent of the developed countries' population will be 65 years and over.

Increasingly referring to itself as the 'young-old' market, marketers predict that this category is set to become the second growth market of the 21st century. The marketing process, however, must start earlier in the demographic cycle. People aged 50 and over is a good place to begin as they are an increasingly influential market to be targeted by companies. Freed from the costs of mortgages and child rearing, approaching early retirement full of zest, both mentally – and, increasingly, because of improved health care – physically, they are also more financially prosperous as a result of the widespread inheritance of first-generation home-owners to pass on their properties to children. Many are now 'empty-nesters': the children are raised and have flown from the family home. They now indulge in travel – taking 2.5 times more trips than other demographic groups – a point that has already been capitalized by the travel and airline industries in satisfying their thirst for leisure; they already represent 30 per cent of the total tourism market world-wide.

The consumption potential is compelling. Americans over 55 years, for example, account for about half of all discretionary spending, a proportion that is set to rise as the population ages. With purchasing power 30 per cent above other demographic groups, this group represents an enormously potential market as many marketers discover a particularly alluring trait: their attitude towards spending. Generally, satisfied with their standard of living, most people over 55 years in the USA either own their homes, or have paid off their mortgage. They have also financed their children's education and still have reserves for presents for the grandchildren, travel, leisure and re-decoration. The fact that they have achieved top income levels in their pre-retirement age and are seemingly content to spend what they earned and enjoy life while they have it should be an attractive element to retailers and marketers.

But seasoned marketers familiar with this group are more circumspect; while the 'young-old' may have the disposable income, they don't easily part with it. They have earned their income over a life-time of industry, and are not likely to transform themselves into spendthrift customers now. They share a general trait for continued bargain hunting and buying from discount stores – in spite of their discretionary spending habits. A life-time of shopping experience makes for careful, and sometimes hesitant, buying decisions. People in the elderly category need even more details, quality assurances and transparent evidence that add up to compelling reasons to buy.

Marketing implications

In global marketing terms, it's not really that this group has been overlooked so much as that it has been neglected. The marketing process needs to rapidly adapt to exploit the demographic opportunities earlier in the pre-retirement cycle if loyalties are to be forged.

The neglect of this demographic group has been more conspicuous amongst the retail trade. Many have bypassed opportunities by not transforming and differentiating their stores to distinguish between a customer service for time-conscious, younger two-earner householders and another for the older 'empty-nest' couple. Surveys in the UK in the early 1990s showed that more than half the over-55s segment thought that clothes stores did not really cater for people of their age. 60 per cent of those surveyed said that stores were not able to advise on the products sold. DIY retailers, in particular, stand to gain by more careful market segmentation and differentiating themselves by concentrating on home decoration, repair and improvements, etc and training staff to cater for this category of client.

UK brewers are starting to reposition their properties to reflect a less male-oriented, boozing club image, towards values and attractions that cater for, *inter alia*, older people out for a lunch time snack. Inns and pubs will evoke an image of being clean and comfortable without being ostentatious, and serve meals at all times during the day. The beverages offered will also change, with innkeepers providing more soft drinks, non- and low-alcohol beers and coffee, to appeal to the more health-conscious older clientele.

The over-65 year-olds – many of them in single-person households – should not be neglected either, as a potential market. In the USA, the 1990 census showed that the over-65s group was in excess of 31.3 million, an increase of 22 per cent from 1980.

This ageing affluent group provides potential markets for luxury items like cosmetics and cars. Predictably, anti-ageing cosmetic products also feature highly on their buying list. In Japan – the fastest-ageing country – cosmetic companies are devoting more than half of their annual R & D budgets to studying the secrets of youth. In a country with a unique mixture of ageing post-war baby boom (15 per cent of the population is over 65) and a current birth rate decline (9.6 births per 1,000 people), Shiseido, Japan's largest indigenous cosmetic company, has developed a range of 90 successful anti-ageing creams. Cosmetic and toiletry product manufacturers have also noted the older market is quite *coquette*: they spend on average two hours in the bathroom compared to 20 minutes by their juniors.

Today, luxury car buyers tend to be about ten years older and more affluent than the average car buyer is. But this is not confined to luxury models. The increasing significance of the older groups suggests that cars should be developed specifically for this age group. Standard model car manufacturers have discovered that older drivers retain their vitality considerably longer than was formerly the case and tend to want to maintain their life-styles they have grown fond of, for as long as possible. Far from considering a diminished level of social activities, they demonstrate astonishingly high rates of mobility. Increasingly over-65s use their car for excursions and visits to friends, and use it for more than half their journeys.

To attain a favourable competitive position amongst the older population, car manufacturers need to accelerate preparations for this market in the future by inconspicuously adapting their vehicles to their special needs: older people have higher requirements in respect of comfort and of safety of function and service, but a reduced ability to digest complex technologies and a reduced level of physical agility.

But courting this segment of the population has proved tricky for many marketers. Companies making a concerted effort to target this group have tended to adopt one of three marketing approaches:

- offer price reductions
- devise a separate marketing strategy for this group, or
- make their sales and marketing 'ageless'.

The first approach is employed by many service industries, by offering 'senior citizen' rates for public transport, cinemas, sporting events and cultural attractions. A separate promotional pitch aimed at the older market has been used successfully by the travel industry. Club Med, for instance, launched a 'Forever Young' programme to select destinations. Part of the attraction of this programme was the emphasis on socializing: people over 55 years showed an interest in mixing and meeting people of all ages from many parts of the world, a theme which was exploited by creating a congenial and secure setting in their properties throughout the USA. Locations have been adapted to provide appropriate shopping facilities, organized excursions and golf facilities. Stairless, comfortable accommodation added to the attraction, together with low-calorie, no-fat and vegetarian meals, although this also cuts across an increasingly large segment of the population.

Another enlightened example of marketing adaptation to respond to changing demographics comes from an unlikely source: ice-cream manufacturers. Faced with markets in the developed countries characterized by fewer children and more older people, ice-cream manufacturers envisage selling more elaborate products that can compete with other forms of desserts and snacks for older customers. Included in the new strategies is the emphasis of ice-cream parlour chains, frequently owned by the suppliers, like Allied Domecq in the UK and Dairy Queen in the USA.

From the marketing communications' perspective, the key pitfall has been the use of the wrong term 'old' to describe this segment. This is now giving away to a more socially correct parlance in marketing campaigns, which emphasizes the third approach – the promotion of an ageless theme. Cosmetic firms adopted the ageless notion in reaching this segment based on a positioning underlining that beauty had nothing to do with age or about looking young. This was visually reinforced by featuring role-models of the age group and deleting words in ads like 'younger looking' as a positive adjective. Recurrent themes and products features which have proven successful with over-65s tend to focus on changes in life-style, health status and outside interests.

Two additional characteristics of the over-65 demographic group require attention in devising new products and building an appropriate dialogue with this segment: they are increasingly living alone and are more conscious of their health.

In the USA, statistics underline this phenomena.

■ Elderly women far outnumber elderly men and now nearly half of women over 65 are widowed. Over 65-year-olds account for 40 per cent of all single-person households and similar trends are emerging in Europe.
■ Older people, helped by improved health care and advice, are taking a bigger interest in healthier eating as they get older. More attention is paid to food advertising to identify the healthiest opportunity that will deliver more energy to pursue their pleasure interests. Fast-food and convenience foods (time-saving devices) may not be an attractive prospect for customers of this age group.

An increasingly health-conscious population is not only an American phenomenon. In Europe, better-balanced diets have resulted in an overall rise of two years in the region's life expectancy since the 1980s, and an increase of ten years since 1970. Broadly similar life-style patterns and consumption needs have emerged in Europe amongst this group, but marketing programmes have remained focused on younger markets. For a variety of reasons, marketing people retain the illusion that the so-called 'grey generation' has evolved to a stage in their life where the only products and services it seems to need are health-related and high-fibre foods. Part of the problem, say some observers, is that advertising people are creating advertisements that mirror themselves – not a surprising revelation since many ad people are under 35. Exploiting the potential in the ageing market requires more elaborate thinking by the marketing function about the demographic profile and shape of the current market, to:

- determine if there is an over-reliance on the youth market to the detriment of other demographic groups
- identify potential amongst the mobile 55-plus group and provide a more adapted level of customer service at the 'point-of-sale'
- avoid alienating the over-65 group by devising a socially correct and 'ageless' approach to winning their loyalty.

THE BABY-BOOMERS

The 'baby boom' represents that bulge in the population born in the late 1940s to the early 1950s. The first wave of the West's post-baby boom has crossed the great demographic divide and is moving inexorably towards middle age, creating what many now refer to as the 'middle-aged youth'. By the end of this century, the middle-aged baby-boomer will represent the largest segment of the population in the developed world. All things being equal, the pattern is set: over 10 million females and a similar number of males in the USA will be middle-aged by 2000. Globally, there are currently 77 million American baby-boomers, many of whom transcended the 1960s-1980s as teddy boys, beatniks, hippies and yuppies. They also made the 1980s the decade of the upwardly mobile group, as millions launched careers, earned and spent real money for the first time in their lives. They also heralded in the two-earner household existence, where both the husband and/or partner held remunerated employment.

A prosperous market segment

The future prospects of this group are compelling for marketers world-wide. The bigger the group grows, the richer it is expected to become as property is inherited by the next generation. By the year 2000, nearly 15 million households will be headed by the 35-54-year-olds who will account for 56 per cent of all consumer spending in the USA. In the UK, it makes up 14 per cent of the population but accounts for one- quarter of household expenditure, representing $750 billion in 1996. In France, they account for 20 per cent of spending on goods and services. Being the largest group of any previous generation, it is expected to constitute around 35 per cent of the world population by 2005, up from 26 per cent today.

As a distinct market segment, the group is also fragmenting as quickly as it is increasing in absolute numbers. The desire for individuality and to be different from one's peers will become more strident than in the past, heightened by increased affluence. But the existence of a more affluent group may not necessarily translate into a desire to consume even more products. Mass-marketing is beginning to be less effective in reaching this group, as demonstrated by the gaps emerging in the food market, created by growing affluence and the baby-boomers' demand for greater differentiation, quality and convenience.

But they are also ageing...

While consumption in the developed world has been dominated by the baby-boomer generation based on two-income families, conspicuous buying by the few on cars, clothes, a borrowing culture and an upwardly mobile culture, they are also ageing. These once free-spending couples have evolved to being serious-minded parents. Having children has reduced both their discretionary income and their spare time. On a world-wide scale, baby-boomers' priorities are changing: they are spending their money on school fees for their children, retirement plans and nursing care for their parents.

Their homes are a reflection of changed times: house ownership is on the increase throughout the EU and USA, albeit in favour of more practical and modest abodes. The transformation towards smaller families has contributed to this trend. Spending behaviour has now shifted to mortgages, home decoration, utility bills and other housing costs, followed by transportation ($1 out of every $5 goes on buying a car or paying for another form of transportation in the USA) and, lastly, purchases of food. Given the fast-paced life-style of this group, convenience eating has proven to be very popular: 46 per cent of all food expenditure in the USA goes on home-delivered food and take-away foods.

The consumerism and excess of the 1980s have given way to conservatism and thrift, but there are other factors at work. The baby-boomers no longer want to shop *ad nauseam*; they have less time to do so. They show less acquisitive behaviour when out shopping and demand more value for money. Sociologists assert that after the 1980s spending spree by baby-boomers, they have reached their 40s and have most of the products they need to live a comfortable life-style.

Increased prosperity has, however, translated into an increase in baby-boomers' saving propensity behaviour. A 1993 US Congress Budget Office study found that baby-boomers were much better prepared for eventual retirement than their parents were at the same age, and could look forward to a generally comfortable retirement early next century. The conclusion was based on the assumption that baby-boomers would reduce their housing assets as they grew old, something that the current generation of elderly had failed to do.

Changing life-styles

Leisure time is now the most coveted asset amongst US baby-boomers. The mid-1980s Louis Harris survey of US life-styles noted that the average weekly number of leisure hours, in an active sense, had dropped from 20 in 1973 to 16 in 1988. Baby-boomers who willingly slaved away during the 1980s – when a 60-hour week almost became a status symbol – now have families and are demanding more time away from the office. Some have opted for a simpler life, thereby creating a phase known as 'down-shifting'. Labour statistics show that the trend has started to take place in the USA: employees clocked up 18 minutes less per week during the first nine months of 1996 than in 1989. The changed life-style is also manifested in better eating to keep the cholesterol counts down, and the increased desire for more leisure time is spent on outdoor activities like picnics, fishing and golf.

The 1990s' downsizing mode and the forced death of the corporate man – the life-time commitment of workers to a single employer – made itself felt predominately amongst the baby-boomer generation. It was to change their perception of life; today, the baby-boomer can expect to have held an average of ten jobs in a life-time and change careers three times.

Marketing implications

The trends described above carry a strong marketing message for companies seeking to address this group. As an increased number of people turn 50 – estimated at a rate of one every seven to eight seconds in the USA – a potential problem for marketers stands out: the baby-boomers have a notorious tendency to reject the notion of growing old. A major rethinking of the demographic definitions in the marketplace is required: simplified notions of the baby-boomers being one homogeneous prosperous group of 30-something consumers is no longer valid. Advertising messages now downplay the ageing process associated with this group and adapt their communications to fit in with their continuing desire to gravitate to youthful images of themselves. At the same time, marketers need to avoid the risk of alienating the youth market. Many view the boomers' children as important emerging markets for a range of products like cosmetics, films and snack foods. As in the case of the older groups discussed earlier, companies need to fine-tune their product positioning and promotional messages and be more discriminatory in customer-service terms if they want to retain both market segments.

Loyalty towards brands, in sharp contrast to the youth market, remains elusive for the baby-boomers: brand names are only as valuable as the goods and services they represent and are likely to be chosen after other brands have been considered. Patronizing TV advertisements are not likely to work with baby-boomers, who were the first generation to grow up with television. In short, the baby-boomers are more discerning and discriminating about brands and the way they are communicated over the media.

Some companies have adapted their product offerings for this group with success. One leading toothpaste manufacturer created a cocktail of the whitener, Peroxide, and baking powder product, to appeal to baby-boomers with yellowing teeth. The world's leading soup manufacturer, facing the middle-aged American baby-boomers' desire to increasingly eat out instead of making meals at home, re-vamped its product by adding new flavours, improving recipes and offering 'healthier' soups with less salt and fat. In the UK, multi-leisure centres with multiplex cinemas, fast-food outlets, bowling and other activities, have proven a success amongst this group with children, fitting in with the emerging leisure habits. Pressures on time and safety fears have contributed to baby-boomers spending more time at home, but when they do go out, they tend to look for an integrated leisure pursuit, suitable for the whole family.

With the older baby-boomer tending to spend less on retail items and more on financial services, holidays, restaurants and entertainment, retailers will need to think of ways to capture more of this incremental spend by making themselves more attractive to the consumer: more innovative shopping opportunities, home delivery, electronic commerce, etc.

As the male baby-boomer hurtles towards middle age, the choice of media to reach this population will require more careful analysis. Reading habits of this group have changed. General-interest men's magazines in the USA and the more specialized cen-tre-fold, pin-up variations have recorded declining sales. Concerned about getting old, putting on weight and losing their sex appeal, the baby-boomer has turned to men's magazines offer-ing more practical information about health, fitness and grooming. In a world where they compete with women in the workplace, share increasingly in the family-raising role and care more about leisure time, health and appearance, articles featuring balancing one's life now replaces the macho role image that many men's magazines portrayed in the past. The growth of men's life-style magazines and specialist health and fitness titles, like GQ and Men's Health, have been significant. In the USA, Men's Health now sells at 1,400,000 copies a month, while in the UK it was outselling general interest men's titles such as GQ and Esquire 12 months after its launch.

Surveys show that the prime media for reaching baby-boomers is TV and newspapers, as they spend a substantial amount of time at home. With a tendency to read at least one newspaper a day, they will pay more attention to press adverts than inserts and fliers.

Getting the marketing right for the baby-boomer segment is no longer a simple affair as it was in the past. They have aged, show a dislike for shopping sprees and spend more time at home. A study of the value systems associated with the baby-boomer population also shows that while relatively more prosperous, giving them a sense of financial well being and being unique individuals, baby-boomers do not always share the same attitudes towards work, leisure time and accumulating assets as their parents. Surveys indicate that they share a number of values as a group that contrast significantly with those of the previous generation.

■ Experiences are just as important as possessions. Baby-boomers tend to feel that going through interesting experiences is more rewarding than material possessions or fighting their way up the corporate ladder. They see experiences as a means of broadening themselves. In a 1988 Harvard Business School survey 47 per cent of baby-boomers responded that personal development was the second most important thing in life next to their family.

■ Unlike their parents who looked upon work as an obligation, baby-boomers expect to have fun at work; social contacts, opportunities to learn new skills, travel, exercise and mobility all feature highly on their list. Work that is not enjoyable leads to unproductive contributions and a desire to seek alternative employment. Although the recession and corporate downsizing of the 1980s and early 1990s may have curtailed this aspiration, many moved to flexible work schedules and working from home as a means of adding a challenge to their lives. Today the home-based workforce is set to be one of the fastest-growing components of the US and European labour market.

■ Better education and more opportunities to study after school than their parents, has led the baby-boomers thinking of themselves as professionals; they hold the expectation that they should be treated as such. They are 'professionalizing' many roles that were not considered professional positions. Having said that, they wish to develop all aspects of themselves beyond the work environment. Their identities are linked less strongly to their careers than were their parents, whom they considered did not lead balanced lives because they did not have much of a life outside of work.

THE POST-BABY-BOOMERS

The generation following the baby boom – those born after 1964 – are coming of age, but there are fewer of them and their economic impact is not as easy to determine at this stage.

In marketing terms this group of young people, the oldest of them being 33 or 34, represents an entry of new consumers which was projected to fall in the 1980-2000 period. According to Peat Marwick McLintock, the international accountants group, the European continent will have 25 per cent fewer 15-24-year-olds by the end of this century, compared to 37 per cent more middle-aged people in the USA. Other surveys predict that the youth market will similarly diminish (see Table 3.1).

Table 3.1 *The diminishing youth market*

	%
Japan	- 2
USA	-8
France	-15
UK	-26
Germany	-37

Lower birth rates after the euphoria of the post-war period to 1964 has resulted in fewer young people coming on stream to fill vacant posts, consume products and services; skill shortages are now a familiar sight in many developed high-tech economies. While the European population grew by 63 million in the 1980s, it progressed demographically less in the 1990s. In the 1980s there was a dramatic drop in the 15-25-year-olds in Germany as their ratio to the population as a whole decreased from 17.5 per cent to 11.5 per cent. These trends continue to haunt the retail trade in the UK, where there has been a 12 per cent decline in the 20-30 age group over the 1990s, hitting sales of youth fashions and chart music, as well as products associated with first-time households like furniture and DIY.

Many economists, armed with upbeat forecasts in the 1980s, thought that as these young people entered the workforce, their relative shortage would put upward pressure on their wages. Instead, their pay has fallen, creating wage differentials between themselves and the baby-boomers. Some economists are less pessimistic. The youth market, they argue, could continue to be attractive to marketers because its buying power is only partly covered by its own income – parents and grandparents emerged as being sponsors of this group and have significantly increased the buying capacity of this consumer group.

In the longer term, the key question is whether the post-baby-boomers will eventually be able to earn enough and spend enough to keep the market prosperous. In the USA, property agents are already predicting that house values are not expected to increase beyond inflation for the next few decades as smaller generations of the post-baby boom follow their predecessors into the housing market.

Like the previous demographic groups, the post-baby-boomer group is not a mass-homogenized cluster. Marketers see two distinct categories within this segment:

The 30-something-generation

This category, often as parents of young children, have tasted the affluence of the consumer boom of the mid-1980s and will probably retain all its self-possession and self-obsession, taking its buying habits with them beyond the end of the century. Many of the youth products will follow them up the age structure. These people will still listen to popular music, albeit on compact disks rather than stereo record players. Clothes groups in the UK have started to adapt their style of garments to appeal to this group to reflect a range of clothing which will be less fashion-led but still stylish with designer appeal. Another feature of this group – different metabolism – has led to clothing manufacturers offering wider waist bands and ampler fittings.

Marketing people targeting their products at this group will find that the 30-something-market shares common characteristics throughout Europe: single owners of their homes, employed in the community, social or in the personal services sector, and owning at least one TV set, according to Euromonitor market analysts. In a sweeping survey of 23 countries in 1994, the key characteristic found amongst this group was increased home ownership – now accounting for 55 per cent of the households in Europe – and a heavy skewing towards single-person households. In Scandinavia and Germany, for example, single people occupy a third of all homes.

The 20-somethings or the New Wave young

These are the first children of Reaganomics and the policies of the EU. They are, above all, the first group to grow up in the service- and consumption-led information society and their exposure to communications technology that has shaped their values and expectations.

Less wedded to their jobs, they are much more mobile and less motivated by money. Falling birth rates from the early 1970s onwards has resulted in fewer consumers in this group (see Table 3.2). They are now in a position to make demands on their employ- ers that previous generations never would have dreamed of. A sur- vey of 1,000 US college students showed that starting salary ranked sixth in importance in a list of job considerations; oppor- tunity for promotion came in first place.

Table 3.2 *Birth rates: older generations not being replaced as the declines average number of children per woman*

Country	1970	1994
Belgium	2.25	1.55
Denmark	1.95	1.80
Germany	2.03	1.26
Greece	2.39	1.35
Spain	2.90	1.22*
France	2.47	1.65
Ireland	3.93	1.86
Italy	2.42	1.22*
Netherlands	2.57	1.57
Finland	1.83	1.85
Sweden	1.92	1.88
UK	2.43	1.74
EUR-15	2.38	1.45
USA	2.02	2.08
Japan	2.10	1.50

* Estimate.
Sources: Eurostat, United Nations World Population Prospects, 1994.

As the developed world produces fewer people between 10 and 20 (see Table 3.3), their coming of age as a smaller demographic group may yet prove to be as strong an influential force on work, leisure and social values as the baby-boomers. This group is exceptionally brand-aware: they buy and display brands to express a personal, individual sense of style and self-expression. But this is not to say that they are acutely image- and status-conscious consumers, like their predecessors the baby-boomers at the same age. Overt consumerism does not feature highly in their priorities. While marketers previously focused on consistency to build brand values, manufacturers now have to say something that is currently relevant and interesting, rather than just consistent. This means more frequent new campaigns. With buying habits more of a casual affair, it is natural for them to acquire durables and dispose of them just as quickly.

Table 3.3 *World population aged 10-20: declining birthrates, fewer customers*

Year	World		Developing countries		More developed countries	
	(mn)	(%)	(mn)	(%)	(mn)	(%)
1975	1,906	46.7				
1995	2,289	40.3	2,064	42.9	222.0	25.9
2000	2,367	39.0	2,147	41.4	220.0	25.0
2005	2,401	36.6	2,188	39.5	215.0	24.1
2015	2,421	33.6	2,217	35.6	204.0	22.3

Source: World Bank.

Within this group there is evidence of fragmentation on an international scale making it even more difficult to reach them with the standard marketing formats of the past. Individualism may emerge as being the common thread to categorize this group but is subject to different interpretations in different foreign markets. Four psychographic categories amongst this young adult population were found to exist world-wide following a survey conducted of the 30-something group by WPP's advertising research arm.

- Enthusiastic materialists – found largely as a phenomenon in the emerging markets of China, Africa and India, they consist of groupings enthusiastically adopting western values, showing a desire to outwardly demonstrate material trappings of status and success. Impatient to earn money, they are not prepared to spend years making progress like their parents.

- Complacent materialists – a largely Japanese trait also found in mature markets where young adults subscribe to the new moderation: a more balanced life-style between home and work, confident that they will prosper without little effort.
- Swimmers against the tide – describes those struggling to maintain material ambitions in the face of economic downturn. Life has become a vicious circle of having to work hard to maintain a life-style they aspire to – but have no time to enjoy it.
- New realists – found in many mature markets of the Northern Hemisphere and led by the view that they are never going to achieve the material affluence of their parent's generation and have amended their goals accordingly.

Marketing implications

The post-baby-boomers are proving to be elusive TV viewers. The three largest US TV networks found in the mid-1990s that the youth audience, who are their key audience and attractive to advertisers, had turned to cable channels or the Internet which presented more compelling interests for them. Prime-time audience saw its share tumble from 23 per cent in the 1993-4 season to 16 per cent in 1995-6. Two years of copycat programming in a desperate fight for the young audience helped to regain the ground lost, but with one undesirable outcome: the networks disenfranchised their older audiences.

Many advertisers are finding that this generation of young adults requires different 'levers' for message communication. Humour, if relevant to the local culture, and approaches which reflect consumers' own values and life-styles are found to be engaging. Reaching these young adults will prove difficult with traditional marketing approaches as they are not as gullible as their predecessors in the face of stereotyped images and despise overplay of 'hip' notions. But the marketing approach must go far beyond simply communicating with the young adults; it also involves repositioning the product and frequently modifying the offerings to reach and retain this clientele. The issue can be complex when the company's products appeal to more than one demographic group.

The case of one US fast-food company illustrates how complex this problem can be across the baby-boomer and young-adult markets. For many years, the company had defined its target market only in broad demographic and psychographic categories, in accordance with its generic mass-market orientation: very frequent consumers (VFCs) of its fast-food products aged between 13 and 24 purchased and consumed on the premises. Marketing people had convinced senior management that to appeal to this range of consumers additional food items should be offered at the outlets throughout the country. After years of such a practice, the company's attempts to keep everyone happy became increasingly difficult and costly.

A more refined study of the customer base revealed that it consisted of three distinct groups: those who visited the outlets at least once weekly, those who visited as little as once monthly and those who had visited the outlets only once but would not repeat the experience as they didn't like fast-food. Significantly, two of these distinct groups stood out as being high-potential customers.

- Cost-conscious customers: 18-24-year-olds who visited the outlets frequently but with a limited budget, thus spending modestly and buying on average three-four items from the least-priced menus.
- Time-conscious customers: slightly older baby-boomer-type clients characterized by harassed two-earner couples or parents concerned with quick service, ease of use but sensitive to taste and quality; they visited the outlets less frequently and purchased higher-priced menus.

Armed with this information, and struck by the realization that the two segments represented 70 per cent of turnover but made up less than 30 per cent of the customer base, the company re-positioned its offerings to appeal to both groups. For the time-harassed clients, a speedy service was launched and an on-demand programme introduced to reduce waiting times; the cost-concerned younger clients were attracted by a better choice of items taken from the core menu offerings and reduced in price.

The younger cost-conscious consumer may not, however, remain a penny-pinching individual forever. Private banks in the key European centres have targeted part of this segment of the population with whom relationships can be built over the long term: the young educated adult who will go on to be professional like doctors who, while not having fortune now, have the potential to acquire one. Typically they have started a high-income career but still may have nothing in the bank. In the major financial centres around the world, this category of the young professional is pursuing lucrative careers. Marketing analysts view this group as eventually becoming good at making money, but with no experience at handling it. Banks have lured them on the basis that they represent future wealth based on the high-income career they have embraced and, frequently, will become in time part of a two-earner high-income household. Some banks believe that the pattern of wealth is, in any event, changing throughout Europe as inheritance will become less important relative to people who are building up their own wealth. While starting with modest deposits, the young-achievers' segment will be guided by private banks as they grow older: the goal is to manage debt and assist them change over time from a banking relationship to an asset management relationship. For those banks pursuing such clientele, it has evolved from targeting 'old money' to 'new money', albeit a new class of customers, 'no money – yet'.

Whatever the future holds in terms of their consumption patterns, there is general consensus amongst experts on two facts.

- The decline in the number of young people could boost their spending power if labour shortages translate into higher wages. The youth market could be quantitatively smaller but more affluent.
- After 30 years of over-reliance focused on the youth market, retailers and manufacturers alike have realized that the teenager category may remain in any event a declining part of the market. The need to appeal to other age groups is essential, with a differentiated product and communications strategy.

In the longer term, other economists have raised the concern that as people live longer and work for a shorter time, whole generations under 35 will have to consume less and save more during their working lives. In Europe and the USA, as we saw above, governments are faced with problems about how to provide for ageing populations. The immediate issue is that there is a declining number of people of working age in a position to pay taxes and national insurance in order to support the fast-growing population of retired people. A new type of retirement savings scheme – the 'stakeholder pension' – is being envisaged, providing greater flexibility of saving through personal and company pension schemes. Unless alternative steps are taken and the birth rates increase, the impact into the next century will be shouldered largely by the post-baby-boomer generation, as they plough a greater proportion of their disposable income into pensions.

Another concern expressed by many is the effects of technological change which has made it increasingly difficult for corporations – and governments – to commit themselves to long-term employment. As IT costs drop, people are becoming an expensive optional component. Even when displaced, people find alternative work often at lower rates of pay, to a point were some economists are warning of the impact of exchanging of well-paid manufacturing jobs for poorly-paid service jobs. The result may be that many people will no longer be the consumers they used to be.

THE WORKING FEMALE MARKET

Major changes have occurred in the role of the female in society. The most visible change is the growth in the female work participation. The immediate reason for this renewed interest in the working female, according to some observers, is that economic growth has created skilled labour shortages coupled with more casual, part-time work, on top of the demographic fact of falling numbers of young people. But other deeper social forces are at work. Not only do women form 80 per cent of the projected rise in the UK workforce this decade, but the long-term shift towards service employment also favours them. Young wives constitute a transitional generation caught between the traditional values, on the one hand, which teach them that a woman must have children in order to be fulfilled and that her place is at home, and the desire to participate occupationally in society and business, on the other. This clash, fuelled in the 1970s in part by college-university experiences, has created a 'Shakespeare to diapers' syndrome. Manufacturers understood belatedly in the early 1980s what was happening and launched an entirely different range of convenience products and services, distancing themselves from the 'cornflake family' era of the 1970s.

- By 1995, 61 per cent of all women with children under 18 years in the USA were in the workforce, compared to 46 per cent in 1975. This represents nearly half of all working women in the USA. When part-time and full-time jobs are taken into account,

75 per cent of US women now hold some form of salaried occupation. In the EU states, it is expected that by the year 2000 some 87 per cent of all women over 18 years will be in the same situation.

■ Female participation in the workforce has accelerated over the 1990s. 60 per cent of US families have two or more wage earners – most of the new wage earners have been women since 1990. This has been accompanied by a decline in fertility rates in the 1980s, with women having children later in life and fewer of them, and those women entering the workforce doing so earlier and continuing working after they have had their children (Table 3.4).

Table 3.4 *Working mothers with fewer children: in the USA, 61 per cent of females with children under 18 years of age are employed*

Status	One child (%)	Two children (%)	Three children (%)	Four+ children (%)
Stays at home	35	36	18	11
Works half-time	41	37	15	6
Works full-time	48	36	12	4

Source: Interep Research (1996).

■ There are 8 million married working women in the USA who are still living with their husbands and have children under six, representing 63 per cent of all women with children that age.

The working female phenomenon is throwing up different spending and shopping habits that cannot be ignored. Women have less time to shop than they used to. Holding down a job as well as doing the household chores and taking care of children leaves little time for anything else. Surveys show that 30-49-year-old Americans have less than 15 hours of leisure time a week. US women have halved their visit to shopping malls over the past 15 years; and when they do visit, they shop in a more targeted way, entering fewer stores.

Demographically, the 35-44-year-old working female represents the bulk of the market but many manufacturers still haven't re-positioned their campaigns beyond the 18-30-year-olds. The most striking example is in the clothing business at the retail end, where profits have plummeted and store closures are now a daily event in many parts of the developed world. This part of the market has suffered from a decline in fashion-oriented items. These trends are universally similar in key markets like France, where just over 5 per cent of household budgets are spent on clothes, Italy (8.6 per cent), Belgium (7.8 per cent), Japan (6.9 per cent), and near-all-time lows in the USA and UK of 7.3 per cent. There has been a dramatic shift since the 1980s when everyone was concerned how they looked and the focus was on clothing and being fashionable. Lack of time and changing social trends have contributed to less attention being paid to fashion. Designs more suited to the younger female added to the general frustration by the female market as they turned away to spend their money on other items. Demographic trends have simply skewed the population towards older females: women between 35 and 44 years increased by 36 per cent in the period 1980 to 1988, whereas the 14-24-year-old group fell by 13 per cent. Put in marketing terms, there were not enough specialist shops or mail-order catalogues targeted at the older female market.

The changing metabolism patterns of this age group also played a role in lost opportunities by clothes manufacturers: American women in their 30s and 40s weighed about 20 pounds more than they did in their late teens. The 1990s saw the surge in popularity of such products as diet foods, skin creams and close identification with role models that demonstrated that ages 40 and 50 could be attractive.

If the working female is now earning and spending her own funds, studies also reveal that she is increasingly involved in the financial decision-making role at home – a factor that initially eluded the financial institutions. While husbands tend to have the greatest say in financial decisions, wives assert themselves more. Banks and insurance companies have switched their approach and pay more attention when devising strategies for credit card usage, choice of household insurance and investment accounts. In the USA, jewellery retailers are now aiming more marketing effort at women, reflecting the demographic and social shift that has occurred in the past decade: women now have more disposable income and are waiting longer to get married. This so-called 'self-purchase market' for jewellery by women represents 70 per cent of all women's gold jewellery sales in 1996, compared to an estimated 50 per cent in the 1980s.

The contemporary working female is also an avid traveller: estimates suggest that at least one in every five business travellers is a woman. But surveys show how disenchanted they can be in terms of the service provided: nearly half of women executives who travel said they felt that airline cabin crew gave them less attention. A third felt that crews assumed that because they were women they would not mind sitting next to children.

Weekly shopping is no longer the sole prerogative of the woman: women still shop for an average of four hours per week in the UK, but men now share this chore spending an average of two and a half hours per week. Yet many consumer product companies continue to spend most of their advertising budget on attracting women consumers.

THE EMERGENCE OF THE MULTICULTURAL CONSUMER

As the corporate world moves towards the Millennium, further issues face marketing people in the form of diversity of cultures living in most of the major developed economies. Multiculturalism is already a social feature of many countries such as the USA. While marketing may not be a science, attempts to reach the multicultural consumer base is a virtual minefield of complexities. Aside from the language issues discussed in Chapter 2, there are a myriad of uncontrollable factors that can result in lost opportunities.

Most companies have sought out mass-markets of potential customers on the basis of homogenized profiles. The reality is that the markets are also fragmenting in terms of culture as people move across national boundaries in search of new careers, lifestyles and personal aspirations; these concerns go beyond the analysis of demographics described earlier. In the USA, the Asian-American population grew faster than any other racial or ethnic group between 1980 and 1989. Over the same period, the Hispanic population increased by 53 per cent.

Frequently, companies are alerted to the changing cultural composition of their traditional markets through ongoing market research. The most recent example was British Airways, who discovered that 60 per cent of its customers were not British. Its mar-

keting response was twofold: it developed a human resources policy deploying bilingual staff to handle the increasing numbers of
customers whose mother-tongue was not English. More contro-
versially, BA changed the image of its aeroplanes by transforming
the painting on the fuselage from the traditional British red, white
and blue to feature 50 designs from around the world. The positioning drove home the point that the airline was a modern, cos-
mopolitan service provider, with a global reach, more in tune with
the current customer base.

Companies with global ambitions are playing down their national origins and promoting plurality in response to the vast cultural
changes taking place in the world. But communicating with this
multicultural marketplace is also a corporate-wide thrust.
Reaching and retaining these customers means having bilingual
sales staff, in the front-line and customer-service structures. In
predominately bilingual or multilingual environments, staffing
salespeople who speak the customer's language signals that the
company is sincere about its marketing promises. Product features are also important, such as smaller-size clothes for some
groups, products packaged in sizeable quantities for others, etc.

Misplaced advertising and marketing can also miss out on
opportunities amongst ethnic minorities. Research sponsored by
leading UK corporations in 1997 suggested that campaigns were
often misinterpreted or regarded as offensive to ethnic minorities.
While these ethnic groups were still attracted by big-name household brands, care was needed in not using nuances and references
that were properly understood only by people fully integrated into
the country. Equally, the complete absence of ethnic minorities in
many advertisements could alienate minority groups, by suggesting that they were not an integral part of society.

Companies seeking out opportunities in multicultural segments
must do more than simply target these groups. Structures should
include an emphasis on a policy to:

- hire in-house expertise in the culture of the target market with
  the necessary resources and authority to carry out marketing
  plans
- identify an advertising or marketing agency familiar with the
  target market to assist the in-house resources
- carefully research the positioning, communications mode and
  product mixes aimed at the target market

■ integrate the multicultural segments into the overall marketing plan rather than considering it as an incremental source of income.

KEY ISSUES

■ Demographic shifts are taking place on a global scale, affecting consumption patterns and buying behaviour.

■ The markets will consist of older, more single-householders, health-conscious and relatively prosperous consumers.

■ As middle-aged consumers become more prosperous, they will not necessarily consume more of everything.

■ Exploiting profitable opportunities in the future requires a fundamental return to basic marketing principles:

– the constant study and monitoring of the demographic trends in traditional markets served by the company

– the search for cross-selling opportunities in other markets

– focused research of the evolving needs in each market segment and the potential for sustained relationships with the customers throughout the life-cycle

– the creation of focus groups in each demographic segment to guide the company's communications approach and to determine how well the products and services match their expectations.

■ The changing demographics in the marketplace require managing an organizational structural adjustment away from youth to older markets: a shift from mass-market production to flexible processes for increasingly segmented markets.

■ The communications approach should be fine-tuned to each demographic segment and avoid alienating any one sector.

■ Emerging socio-cultural values, such as more part-time work and an orientation towards leisure and the family, is growing in importance in certain developed economies; this has implications for a different marketing approach in product and service offerings – ie pensions, sport/leisure wear, family-type activities, etc.

■ Customers, especially working wives, are spending less time shopping; new ways have to be found to cultivate consumer loyalty that goes beyond the traditional distribution strategies employed by companies.

Positioning of products and services, and the communications mode, has to take account of the multicultural shifts in the marketplace.

BIBLIOGRAPHY

A Adonis and M Suzman, 'So where's the melting pot?', *Financial Times* (20-21 July 1996)

C de Aenlle, 'Going after "no money" class of young professionals', *International Herald Tribune* (15 May 1997)

AMA Management Review, 'Do you know the spenders in your market?' (November 1988)

P Aspen, 'The WASP takes flight', *Financial Times* (16-17 August 1997)

D Bèsenberg, 'Demographic changes in the 90s in Western Europe: opportunities and risks for industry', *European Management Journal*, 7(4) (1989)

N Buckley, 'Retailers face tough time for rest of 1990s', *Financial Times* (23 July 1995)

D Churchill 'A mistake to ignore the female traveller', *Financial Times* (29 June 1989)

W Dawkins, 'Gold streaks highlight Japan's grey waves', *Financial Times* (7-8 January 1995)

The Economist, 'The modest American' (11 February 1989)

The Economist, 'Death and taxes' (13 August 1994)

S Elliott, 'Refocusing ads for aging boomers', *International Herald Tribune* (24-25 December 1997)

P Engberg, 'You can bank on the baby boomers', Scanorama (SAS) (January 1998) European Commission/Eurostat, 'The European Union: key figures' (1997)

S Ferns, 'Trading faces', *Financial Times* How to Spend it Supplement (1997)

P Flanagan 'Don't call 'em old call 'em customers', *AMA Management Review* (October 1994)

V Griffith, 'Missing minutes', *Financial Times* (8 November 1996)

V Griffith, 'Get them while they're young', *Financial Times* (5 January 1998)

D Guinn Mills and M Cannon, 'Managing baby boomers', *AMA Management Review* (August 1989)

W Hall, 'Old-age market reaching maturity', *Financial Times* (30 January 1998)

T Horton, 'The workforce of the Year 2000', *AMA Management Review* (August 1989)

A Jack, 'French fashion trade in deficit', *Financial Times* (5 September 1996)

D Kollat and R Blackwell, 'Direction 1980 – Changing life styles', Management Horizons Inc (1975)

C Leadbeater, 'Dancing to a maturer measure', *Financial Times* (4 January 1990)

L Lutaud, 'Le grand boom des produits "seniors"', *L'Usine Nouvelle* (29 May 1997)

J Lynn, 'Tapping the riches of bilingual markets', *AMA Management Review* (March 1995)

R Martenson, 'Future competition in a cross-cultural environment', *European Management Journal*, 4(3) (1986)

V Matthews, 'Bell tolls for beer and skittles', *Financial Times* (10 February 1997)

H Opaschowski, 'Changing attitudes to work and leisure', Bulletin (Crèdit Suisse) (3rd Quarter 1989)

R Oram, 'Nestlè sales drop 15% in first half', *Financial Times* (21 July 1995)

T Parker Pope, 'All that glitters isn't purchased by men', *Wall Street Journal* (8 January 1997)

C Parkes, 'When the baby boom turned 40', *Financial Times* (24 December 1988)

C Parkes, 'In the end we are big brand people', *Financial Times* (16 January 1989)

R Pogrebin, 'Magazines: Fat? 40? Unhappy? Now men's magazines have the answers', *International Herald Tribune* (10 December 1996)

P Rawstorne, 'Affluence brings European tastes together', *Financial Times* (10 May 1989)

P Rawstorne, 'Why brands must catch the flowing tide of the New Wave', *Financial Times* (11 May 1989)

Research International, 'Are you talking to me? Communicating with young adults' (1995)

Research International, 'Connecting with the baby boomers' (1997)

M Rich, 'Europe's uncommon markets', *Financial Times* (25 August 1994)

Stein Ringen, Citizens, Families and Reform, Oxford: Clarendon Press (1997)

C Russell, 'What's ahead in the 1990s', *New Woman* (January 1989)

R Tomkins, 'Retailers suffer as US loses the urge to shop', Financial Times (22 December 1995)

R Tomkins, 'Campbell Soup preens shaggy dog story', *Financial Times* (10 September 1996)

Verdict Research, 'Verdict on retail demographics'

V de Vezins, 'Le nouvel "ordre dèmographique mondial"', *Le Figaro* (9 August 1994)

M Webb Pressler, 'Hot sales at the high end', *The Washington Post* (26 January 1997)

J Williams, 'Global taste for ice cream', *Financial Times* (20 January 1998)

4

CONTROLLING THE COST OF THE MARKETING ACTIVITY

Tackling marketing costs represents a perennial problem for most corporations. Cost reduction exercises which arbitrarily prune marketing overheads without a real understanding of what is required to support the business only contribute to the internal feuds between marketing and finance, and also damage customer relations.

DETERMINING THE 'RIGHT' BUDGET

Agreeing on determining the 'right' budget for the range of activities associated with the marketing function continues to be the subject of heated debate between marketing and financial heads each year. A number of factors contribute to making this negotiation process more difficult.

The aggregated nature of costs

Marketing appropriations tend to come in chunks of fixed costs. The costs relate more to the provision of big chunks of sales and marketing support capability than the cost of selling a single product. Attempts to apportion the costs over responsibility centres don't make the activities look any more transparent; nor are they made any more controllable as a result. Senior management faces insurmountable problems in attempting to control marketing expenses at this macro-level. Budgets are thus set on the basis of traditional parameters of (1) arbitrary subjective assessments, (2) affordability and (3) a percentage of sales, none of which are suitable in terms of determining the value-added of the marketing activity.

The discretionary nature of the expenditure

The outstanding characteristic of marketing costs is that generally they are incurred to obtain a sale rather than as a result of it. Marketing decisions that generate these costs tend to be discretionary, that is to say, they arise largely from periodic management planning decisions. Problems of control emerge when management begin treating marketing costs like those of a manufacturing operation, which is based on the assumption that overhead costs vary with volume – ie a change in volume 'causes' a change in costs. As the author underlines later, it is misleading to believe that a correlation exists between sales volume and selling/marketing costs, and it is not a valid basis for controlling discretionary costs of this nature.

Compared with manufacturing cost control, corporate controllers are faced with the equally difficult task of measuring marketing costs, thereby rendering *ad hoc* expenditure controls necessary. This task is made difficult because of three factors.

- There are more bases over which to allocate marketing costs. Manufacturing costs are assigned to products and processes; marketing costs can be allocated to such bases or marketing entities as products, customers, territories, size of orders, distribution channels and individual sales staff.
- The decision to allocate marketing costs is more arbitrary. Manufacturing costs – such as material and labour – can be assigned to tangible products. But the basic output of marketing effort is the sales order. It is inherently difficult to identify the specific cost that has contributed to generating different sales' orders.
- The consequences of a decision to alter marketing expenditure are more difficult to determine. The impact of adding another machine on the plant floor is easier to measure than the effect of increased spending on advertising. Equally, the productivity gain/loss of reducing staff levels on a production line has a less tenuous relationship compared to the effect of withdrawing/adding a sales representative in the field.

Thus for a variety of reasons, manufacturing cost accounting techniques, with their emphasis on the setting of standards and the measurement of variances, are not easily applicable to marketing operations in getting to grips with marketing costs.

Misdirected financial controls

Ex post facto financial controls in many companies still rely on basic budget management tools, frequently in an attempt to restrict expenditures (when it's too late). The standard budget tool relies on comparing actual expenditure against budgeted amounts. While measuring the efficiency of the marketing activity (ie staying within the projected budget) it falls short of providing any insight into the effectiveness of the expenditure itself. It also leads to misdirection of management effort. Typically, marketing appropriations are used towards the end of the year to offset shortfalls in profit targets: if profit performance fails to match planned levels, part of the marketing budget is 'readjusted' to ensure the achievement of the short-term profit target.

The dispersed nature of the marketing activity

Ultimately, virtually every activity within an organization exists to service the customer. Aside from production and certain corporate finance activities, a considerable number of diverse corporate activities and processes are associated directly or indirectly with customer fulfilment and are marketing-related. Many of the activities transcend different functional boundaries. Since they are considered as being administrative, sales and marketing overheads, they are rarely analysed as part of the product cost *per se*. Yet, in the USA, marketing costs are estimated to make up more than 50 per cent of the total costs of many product lines, and approximately 20 per cent of the US gross national product (GNP).

Differentiated marketing policy

Policies aimed at product proliferation and market diversification, with sales spread over multiple markets, makes the task of identifying cost factors considerably more complex; each product may be produced in different versions to suit the vagaries of each market, with options, albeit at an additional cost. Many customer groups may be eligible for particular pre-sales service depending on their needs – ie specific packaging and usage instructions, dispersed and low-volume deliveries, focused 'localized' advertising campaigns, etc.

Differentiated marketing in the form of new product variations, separate promotional campaigns, and different package sizes, while contributing to customer satisfaction and a wider customer base, represents a daunting task from the cost analysis perspective.

Weak costing systems

Different products and variations of products to match different customer groups, selling through diverse distribution channels, make significantly different demands on a company's resources. Traditional costing systems do not segregate costs in the same way to differentiate between high- or low-volume products, or distinguish between markets requiring more – or less – tailor-made promotional effort. Above all, staff deployment can vary in each market depending on the magnitude of the marketing tasks to be accomplished. The cost system, however, may not reflect the real burdens imposed by the tasks carried out in each market. The cost data remains aggregated and is of limited value for the purposes of cost analysis and control.

Increased support activities

Contemporary marketing activities have become more diversified, characterized by selling activities spread over a growing number of markets, shortened product life-cycles and multiple brand ranges to cater for different segments. Increased support activity, matching this diversity, is provided by various parts of the organization, such as accounting, IT services, customer services, logistics, quality control, stock handling, production scheduling, etc. All of this adds to the cost of sustaining customer business in the marketplace. In the 1970s, Siemens of Germany estimated that marketing support activities had grown three times faster compared to factory and labour costs. Today, many companies would, intuitively, share Siemens' view.

Misallocation of costs

Companies persist in allocating rising overheads and support costs on the basis of their diminishing direct labour base. This consists of simply spreading these essentially fixed costs across all products flowing through the plant to the customer, thereby reducing the fixed cost per unit – which of course makes the figures look better – but creates a nightmare for cost analysts. The upshot is that firms making more than one product do not know how much they have spent to produce or sell one product, and which products are truly profitable.

While direct labour may no longer represent an adequate measure of resource consumption for cost allocation purposes, overheads arising from IT-intensive operations remain as elusive as the savings it is supposed to generate: substitution of indirect machine costs for direct labour costs can be offset by additional labour-intensive scheduling, quality control and engineering resulting from increased customization of products. In the USA, studies indicate that products made with automative-intensive processes tend not to be charged enough overhead, while products produced conventionally are charged too much because of the additional complexity associated with product diversity.

Overhead costs have traditionally been assigned to products in an arbitrary fashion. Direct labour became the standard basis for cost allocation: if a company deployed 10 per cent of its total workforce to make and sell a product, accountants would simply assign 10 per cent of overheads to the product to determine its costs. The corporate environment has changed. Companies are producing a wider range of products and labour and materials are a declining share of total costs. Shorter product life-cycles, a tendency to buy-in more pre-assembled units and components, and a growth in product proliferation, are now common corporate features. The result is that overhead costs, linked to manufacturing and marketing support activities, have emerged as being a significant cost factor compared to direct labour.

CAPTURING THE TRUE COMPLEXITY OF MARKETING ACTIVITIES

For many years, the absence of analytical tools to trace costs directly to product lines, sales territories, customers or distribution channels did little in helping to identify profitable segments. Some customer groups, for example, demand a lot of attention and thus raise the overall marketing and support costs. If this cost is simply spread evenly across all customers, the most demanding clients will appear most profitable and therefore receive privileged attention. Meanwhile, the less demanding clients, perceived as being marginally profitable, receive less attention by salespeople. Misdirected effort occurs when marketing and support costs are incorrectly allocated to product divisions without examining the real cost and revenue relationship associated with each customer group; a costing tracking mechanism showing who used the resources could reveal whole customer and products groups, previously viewed as being profitable, as loss-makers, and vice versa.

Retailers have begun to understand that not every product or customer group is profitable. By evaluating the true cost of every product or customer order they can ensure that they are not inadvertently cross-subsidizing some customers. An insight into the effort and working capital required for each customer group or transaction, rather than at an aggregate level, is central to maximizing profits in many commodity-type sectors. Matching the labour costs, distribution, stock investments, shelf and warehouse space, with each customer and product group permits a different profitability profile.

The challenge is to find a costing system which mirrors the entire marketing operation, both in the office and in the marketplace, tracing the time, effort and skills needed to market different products in various markets. Improved management accounting systems now permit marketing heads to track more accurately the comparative profitability of different market segments, categories of products and distribution channels and the incremental costs of complexity associated with each. This differs from the traditional approach, which simply lumps all the fixed costs together and re-allocates them in an arbitrary fashion.

But for profitability to emerge, management requires knowledge of the costs of the entire marketing operation – and, indeed, other functions over which marketing people have no control. Product group managers should be concerned with maximizing the spread between costs and revenues to optimize profits; this suggests a reporting system which gives a clear picture of how their products, brands, customers, regions, and distributors contribute to both *generating* revenues and *absorbing* corporate resources.

THE ABC APPROACH

One costing technique that has brought a fresh perspective to this debate in recent years is ABC – Activity Based Costing. This method attempts to segregate the expenses of indirect and support resources by activity and then assigns those expenses based on the drivers of the activities. Proponents of the ABC method argue that resource allocations associated with marketing activities should: (1) explicitly include marketing costs in the costing of products/services and customer groups rather than expensing them over the period, and (2) use a broader set of allocation bases than just sales volume or revenue in the assignment of marketing costs in the first case. The theory behind ABC is disarmingly simple: consider practically all the company's activities as existing to support the manufacturing, marketing and ultimate delivery of products to the customer. By adopting a 'life-cycle' accounting approach – from development to market – this implies that all costs should be:

- identified as product costs
- split apart and traced to individual products or product groups.

ABC seeks to discover the causal factor – the so-called cost driver – which determines the demand for use of a particular overhead resource of the activity. Armed with a knowledge of cost drivers and activity costs, marketing heads can determine overhead allocation rates which can then be re-allocated to specific products, markets or distribution channels. The basis for this allocation is the cost burden individual markets, products, dealers, customers, etc place on these overhead resources.

What drives overheads?

Few managers will dispute the view that demand for some sales overhead resources is directly related to short-term changes in sales volume, such as a targeted sales promotion campaign in a certain region. However, changes in demand for all sales' overhead resources, and thus ultimately in total overhead costs, cannot be fully explained by changes in sales volume.

Changes in demand for some resources can be caused by non-volume-related sales and marketing policy adjustments. For example, the demands placed on accounts receivable, invoicing, after-sales service, etc may be related to the number of these kinds of operations carried out, where they are conducted, for which category of customer and, of course, the scale of the transactions.

ABC sets out to identify the drivers behind each sales/marketing activity to determine the full related cost. The cost drivers provide the best explanation of why costs in an activity change over time. In the case of accounts receivable activities, long-term changes in the cost of the activity pool relating to this task could be related to the number of accounts handled. The number of accounts becomes the cost driver for the activity pool. A cost-driver rate would then be established by determining the number of accounts which the accounts receivable activity is staffed to handle, and dividing this number into the total cost of the activity pool. The outcome establishes a cost per account, which is the absorption rate applicable to each accounts receivable task. This is similar to the way in which labour rates are calculated and applied in a traditional production system.

Tracing marketing expenses to an activity which used these resources and then to individual clients can be very revealing. A leading EU beer manufacturer, frustrated by its inability to control its growing accounts receivable and invoicing expenses, set out to determine what factors created demands on this function and drove its activities. It soon discovered that a sales region with a small number of high-volume clients made significantly less demands on accounts receivable compared to a sales region with fragmented low-volume client base. The company promptly abandoned its traditional allocation base for accounts receivable – ie a uniform percentage of sales – considered to bear no relationship to the activities that generated the administrative work. The reporting system was recast to allocate costs based on responsibility centres, and products, that created the costs.

The ABC methodology elucidates the nature of corporate overhead costs by asking five key questions.

- In the fulfilling a customers' order, developing new business, or handling another customer-related task, how do staff really spend their time – ie form-filling, keying-in data, maintaining customer files, inspecting and expediting customer orders, answering customer inquiries, etc. What interaction is there with other units?

■ Is there considerable waiting around time while processes or orders transcend one department to another? Is there evidence of overtime or reworking because of the complex nature of the customers' requirements?

■ What sort of events or factors initiate these activities? In short, what are the cost drivers? These are factors the occurrence of which creates a cost. The profit centre with low-volume, fragmented client base cited above was a case of a driver (client served by profit centre X) creating a disproportionate demand for an organizational activity (accounts receivable task). Typical marketing cost drivers can be extensive and include the customer type, the promotional resources required and after-sales effort (see Figure 4.1).

Table 4.1 *Marketing cost 'drivers'*

After-sales service effort required
Language and cultural factors in export markets
Customer type – frequent value-added or occasional non-value-added user
Number of customers in sales region
Change in marketing mix
Promotional resources used in each market segment:
administrative backup effort, catalogue selling, store
promotions, commissions, etc.
Sales development needed in opening new markets
Tailor-made or customized products
Distribution channel differences
Market segmentation differentials: geographic, age,
gender income group, bicultural, etc.

■ What do these tasks or activities add in terms of value? Do they have any impact on customer satisfaction?

■ Can a reporting system be devised to reflect the disaggregated cost structures, enabling each function within the marketing department to determine the optimum level of resources needed to carry out its tasks?

The ABC exercise provides an opportunity to identify unnecessary tasks, reporting systems, transactions, space utilization, etc that add no value in terms of quality, use, appearance or customer features. It may reveal duplication of work by two different units within the same product group, and may suggest how changes in one function could result in significant time and cost savings in another. Senior management does not need to wait until an ABC system is implemented before acting on this information. The search for non-value-added activities and wastage in the marketing area can reveal how fruitful such initiatives prove in uncovering potential opportunities for re-deployment of resources. Texas Homecare, a US DIY retailing chain acquired by UK-based Sainsbury's, discovered that 55 per cent of the hours spent by sales staff was not related to anything that happened on the sales floor; it embarked on a campaign to eliminate non-customer-service hours through, for example, the re-design of delivery systems (resulting in a cost reduction of 3 per cent of sales) and wider use of suppliers' own quality checks.

On a broader scale, Matsushita, the world's largest consumer electronics group, examined its cumbersome bureaucratic operations to synchronize its activities in line with customer service needs after it found that only 20 per cent of working hours put in by marketing staff were directly related to business. Much work, both at HQ and within its group companies, was being duplicated. ABC goes further in 'internalizing' the process and building the costing system to provide better information about resource usage.

Getting started

As a preliminary analysis of marketing costs, the ABC technique can be applied in identifying standard marketing costs linked to product lines and territories, as a means of measuring profitability, determining prices or deciding whether to drop product lines and abandon markets. This would involve the following five steps.

■ List all of those activity pools associated with customer fulfilment exercise regardless of department. Clearly, activity chains in most organizations can be long, complex and tangled, cutting across boundaries and looping through functional silos; but they have to be identified as a first step to get an overall picture of what is involved in the normal customer-order cycle. For the sake of simplicity, assume that these activities consist of selling, warehousing, invoicing, packing and delivery and advertising (Table 4.2).

■ Calculate the direct costs of each of these activities and segregate them into variable and fixed categories (see Tables 4.3 and 4.4). A certain degree of subjectivity will be employed in determining the variable versus fixed components of the cost pools.

■ Allocate cost drivers to each activity. For selling, the driver could be orders processed or number of sales calls. For invoicing and accounts receivable, the driver would be the number of orders or number of clients. For order-filling and processing the driver would be the number, weight or size of orders shipped (Table 4.4).

■ Determine the unit cost for each activity. The nominator is the total activity pool cost and the denominator the cost driver selected (Tables 4.3 and 4.4).

■ Prepare a profitability analysis by region (France and UK) and by product (X, Y and Z) (Tables 4.5-4.7).

Approximate accuracy is adopted in this case.

Table 4.2 *Company product line data (French francs)*

	Product lines		
	X	Y	Z
Selling price	10	9	12
Volume units sold and delivered	45,000	30,000	23,000
Average weight of units sold (kg)		2.0	3.0 4.0
Number of customers' orders	150	200	200
Sales revenue	450,000	270,000	276,000

Table 4.3 *Company per unit costs*

Marketing activity	Cost driver	Total volume	Direct cost of marketing activity Total	Unit rate
Selling	Value of sales	996,000	50,000	5.0%
Advertising	Volume of units sold	98,000	40,000	FF0.41
Warehousing	Weight of shipped	272,000kg	27,200	FF0.10
Packing and delivery	Volume delivered	98,000	20,000	FF0.204
Invoicing	Number of customers' orders	550	10,000	FF18.0

Table 4.4 *Variable and fixed costs*

Marketing activity	Variable cost	Unit rate	Fixed cost	Unit rate	Total cost
Selling	30,000	3.0%	20,000	2.0%	50,000
Advertising	15,000	0.15	25,000	0.25	40,000
Warehousing	14,000	0.05	13,200	0.05	27,200
Packing and delivery	12,000	0.12	8,000	0.08	20,000
Invoicing	2,000	3.60	8,000	14.40	10,000

Table 4.5 *Company sales, by region (volume)*

Report by region	Total	X	Products Y	Z
Products sold				
UK	52,000	20,000	12,000	20,000
France	46,000	25,000	18,000	3,000
Total	98,000	45,000	30,000	23,000
Customers' orders				
UK	345	130	130	85
France	205	20	70	115
Total	550	150	200	200
Company sales by weight (kilos)				
	Total	X	Y	Z
UK	156,000	40,000	36,000	80,000
France	116,000	50,000	54,000	12,000
	272,000	90,000	90,000	92,000

Table 4.6 *Company profitability, by region (FF000s)*

	Total company	UK	Region France	Allocation basis
Sales revenue	996,000	548,000	448,000	
less:				
Cost of sales	770,000	462,000	308,000	
Gross margin	226,000	86,000	140,000	
less: Expenses				
Selling	50,000	27,600	22,400	5 per cent of sales
Advertising	40,000	21,300	18,700	FF0.41/unit

Warehousing	27,200	15,600	11,600	FF0.10/kg
Packing and delivery	20,000	10,600	9,400	FF0.204/ unit sold
Invoicing	10,000	6,210	3,690	FF18/ order
Total expenses	147,200	81,310	65,790	
Operating income	78,800	4,690	74,210	

Table 4.7 *Company profitability report, by product line, all regions (FF000s)*

		Product lines			
	Total company	X	Y	Z	Allocation basis
Sales revenue	996	450	270	276	
cost of sales	770	400	150	220	
Gross margin	226	50	120	56	
Less: expenses					
Selling	50	23.0	15.3	11.7	5 per cent of sales
Advertising	40	18.3	12.3	9.4	FF0.41/ unit sold
Warehousing	27.2	9.0	9.0	9.2	FF0.10/kg sold
Packing and delivery	20	9.2	6.1	4.7	FF.204 /unit sold
Invoicing	10	2.7	3.6	3.6	FF18/order
Total expenses	147.2	62.3	46.3	38.6	
Operating income	78.8	(12.3)	73.7	17.4	

Preliminary conclusions

The ABC method begins to reveal interesting information in Tables 4.6 and 4.7. Whereas overall company profitability is positive

(FF78,800) and the two regional markets are making a profit (albeit less pronounced in the case of the UK – ie FF4,690), an analysis by product elicits a different picture: product X shows an operating loss of over FF12,300, when the costs to serve this product group have been identified and allocated to the group. An additional analysis would need to be conducted to examine the cost features of each product line by separate region to further isolate the reasons for this loss.

Can advertising and sales expenses be re-aligned with the regional markets' potential? Salespeople may urge price relief to raise the sales performance in a region to pre-empt competitive activity. In the absence of relevant cost data, senior marketing staff may have difficulties in refusing such a request. Equally, would customers in region X be willing to pay a premium for this 'speciality' product?

A more careful analysis is needed of the factors which influence this company's overheads (advertising, selling, warehousing, packing/delivery and invoicing) and working out what forces 'drive' costs. The ABC method is most effective in cases like the above company, who makes a mixture of high- and low-volume products. Traditional accounting systems show the low-volume products to be highly profitable. Their share of overheads is related primarily to sales volume, and such products often carry a higher price tag than the large-volume items. Despite the copious details of the above traditional P & L analysis, it is inadequate in getting to grips with such questions.

In reality, an ABC analysis would reveal that lower-volume products Y and Z should carry a greater share of the overheads. Why? Because the activities and costs associated with order-taking/processing, warehousing, packing, inspecting, etc and setting up machine's to produce the items usually account for a larger proportion of the products overheads. In addition, a low-volume product may require parts not used elsewhere in the factory or time-consuming sales effort and more elaborate in-store promotion not absorbed by the other products. This imposes a heavy cost burden on certain products, something that is not recognized under traditional costing systems. It is also clear that by using allocation criteria like orders and sales value, they do not always represent an adequate basis for determining resource consumption within the marketing department, or in the factory.

According to Professor Bob Kaplan of the Harvard Business School, an ABC pioneer, the key question that management should be asking, is 'Which parts of the organization tend to grow as the company increases the diversity of its product line, its customer base, its marketing channels?' Intuitively, seasoned marketing professionals, especially those working closely with the customer, know that certain products and customers require more effort (corporate resources) than others; yet the amount of marketing overhead allocated to these products will not reveal the true burden.

To take a simple example, the marketing department may find that the order-taking and processing activity may consume about 80 per cent of the salespeople's time and thus costs £100, 000 in staff cost pa If the 'output measure' is a completed order, ready for delivery, and if 2,000 sales orders are generated on average each year, the order-taking/processing cost per sales order would be £50. The ABC analysis might determine that there is need for two types of measures: simple orders and complicated orders (multiple line entries, complex technical codes, details about variations required by the customer). On the basis of staff costs alone, the simple order might cost £35 and the more complicated order would bear the £75 cost.

ABC – AN ONGOING MEASURE OF PERFORMANCE

Much of ABC analysis has been focused on data from past operations, which diminishes its usefulness as an action-oriented tool for management decision-making.

Coding costs

ABC analysis is perhaps much more meaningful as an ongoing tool for performance monitoring and timely questioning as to why certain marketing actions were taken and what impact will they have on overhead resource consumption. This requires re-casting the accounting information by coding all costs to activities as they are incurred. A methodology for coding costs will have to be devised, requiring staff to fill in time sheets to record the time spent on each activity. In most organizations, staff costs can be the key expense item and it is frequently people in different units throughout the organization who determine the activities to be pursued. The criteria governing the recoding of costs should be simple and follow the broad guidelines shown in Table 4.8 (page 101-2).

Revenues and resources

Tackling the growing aggregate 'fixed-cost' nature of much of marketing activity and the dispersed composition of customer-related tasks across different functions and products, necessitates a finer level of analysis of how the company is generating its revenues and using its resources. Consider the following example of a typical manufacturing company producing three very different products at two plants.[1] Product A is tailored to each customer's specific needs, and products B and C are standard mass-produced items selling at $5 and $10, respectively. Overheads are allocated to products on the basis of labour hours, as in Figure 4.1.

Products	A	B	C	Total
Sales	8,000	3,000	5,000	16,000
Direct materials	1,800	1,000	800	3,600
Direct labour	1,800	500	1,700	4,000
Production				
overhead	1,800	250	850	2,900
Gross profit	2,600	1,250	1,650	5,500

Overheads				
Distribution costs	1,500			
Marketing costs	1,600			
Finance/admin costs	300			
Premises costs	300			
Interest paid	100			
Depreciation	600			
Total overheads	4,400			
Profit before tax	1,100			

Overheads

A cursory glance at the performance of this company on the basis of a traditional P & L analysis would indicate that product A is the most profitable. Beyond that, little information is available about the attributable nature of the overheads, amounting to $4.4 million – ie who used what? In particular, questions need to be posed regarding which product consumed more of the marketing resources – or, indeed, the nature of the distribution policy – resulting in $1.5 million charges for the period. Cumulatively, the controllable overhead costs (excluding interest paid, depreciation and premises) represent 21 per cent of sales, a level which is significant enough to warrant further analysis to identify which activities (products) used what resources (overheads).

The exercise would begin by examining the P & L Statement from an absorption costing perspective – a procedure which charges fixed as well as variable overhead to cost units. The absorption costing analysis based on labour hours in Figure 4.2 suggests that products A and B are profitable but product C has made a loss of $371,000. An initial prognosis would indicate that the loss could be attributed to the labour-intensive nature of the product. But even this more detailed level of analysis does not reveal much by way of information to guide senior management in identifying the true nature of the overheads.

The ABC technique calls for the (1) preparing an extensive list of overhead activities associated with the fulfilment of these sales by product, and (2) the identification of the cost drivers responsible for initiating the activities. The ABC analysis should elucidate the factors behind the global indirect cost of $7.3 million (production overhead of $2.9 million and general overhead of $4.4 million), as shown in Figure 4.8.

Product	A	B	C	Total
Sales	8,000	3,000	5,000	16,000
Direct materials	1,800	1,000	800	3,600
Labour	1,800	500	1,700	4,000
Production overhead	1,800	250	850	2,900
Gross profit	2,600	1,250	1,650	5,500
Labour hours	150 (40.5%)	50 (13.6%)	170 (45.9%)	370 (100.0%)
Overhead	1,784	595	2,021	4,400
Profit	816	655	-371	1,100

Activity	A	B	C	B/C shared	NA (1)
Sales	8,000	3,000	5,000	-	-
Direct labour	1,800	500	1,700	-	-
Direct materials	1,800	1,000	800	-	-
Gross profit	4,400	1,500	2,500		
Attrib. production overhead	1,500	200	700	-	-
Other production overhead	300	-	-	200	-
New client business	100	30	80	-	-
Repeat client business	120	50	60	-	-
After-sales service	30	15	10	-	-
New product development	45	-	50	-	-
Upgrading existing products	5	-	-	-	-
Reporting systems	15	-	-	10	-
Meetings	15	-	-	3	-
Travel	5	-	-	-	-
Sales staff hiring	10	-	-	10	-
Staff appraisals	10	5	5	-	5
Training	15	5	5	-	8
Budget preparation	-	-	-	-	25
A/c rec.	5	5	7	-	-
Warehousing and handling	250	80	150	-	-
Delivery	500	200	320	-	-
Promotion	-	187	-	-	-
Advertising	100	300	500	-	-
Packing	15	5	5	-	-
Depreciat.	300	150	150	-	-

Premises charges	100	-	-	150	50
Quality control	15	5	5	-	-
Interest					100
Total indirect costs (2)	3,455	1,237	2,047	373	188
Attrib. contrib.(3)	945	263	453	-373	-188

(1) Non-attributable overheads
(2) Total indirect costs = $7.3 million
(3) Attributable contribution (profit) = $1.1 million

Who is consuming overhead resources?

By tracing and coding the costs direct to activities and then to the individual products, the ABC analysis in Figure 4.3 provides a slightly more accurate picture of who is spending the overhead resources. More importantly, it gives a penetrating insight into how the funds were consumed and fosters more meaningful questions of a global marketing nature.

■ Why are no funds spent on new product development for product B, and yet products A and C consume £45,000 and $50,000 respectively for this activity?
■ How does management justify meetings costing $15,000 on product A, and only $3,000 between products B and C?
■ Has marketing strategy dictated the marketing effort to be deployed between new clients and repeat client business or does it reflect the initiatives taken by the salespeople?
■ What specific reasons explain the high level of resources absorbed by after-sales service for all products? Does this indicate a more general deficiency in the quality of the product or difficulties encountered by customers in installing the equipment?
■ Does product A have particularly complex delivery schedules or low-volume delivery lots that explains high delivery costs?

Questions relating to other overheads could be probed on the basis of this analysis regarding, for instance, training decisions, centralized budget preparation, stock management and handling procedures, etc. Decisions by the product managers concerning these corporate resources will take on a new dimension, as these will now become overheads, directly billed to the business units, and having an impact on the bottom line. One major contribution of ABC is to highlight the misdirected policy of spreading overhead costs evenly across all products on the basis of labour hours. Even for items like depreciation, there may well be a justification for re-allocating such charges to dedicated and expensive equipment required for a specific process within a business unit, and not resort to spreading the charge equally over all products.

The key thrust is to provide relevant information to bring the costs of the marketing activities to the surface by disaggregating them to direct products which consume resources. Those responsible for individual products are made aware of the cost implications of their decisions. From the perspective of improving resource utilization, the ABC exercise should guide marketing heads in examining four key options.

■ Rationalize, abolish, reduce or outsource activities under their responsibility that add no value in the chain of events that lead to the order fulfilment.

■ No longer consider in-house support services as being a 'free service' to be used when and where they please.

■ Negotiate, for common services used by all product groups, an upper-limit resources budget for these services between the users and suppliers, making the users more responsible for the efficient use of such resources. If they are charged for services, product groups will be urged to consider whether overuse is a problem or if more cost-effective sources exist outside the organization.

■ Promptly address *ad hoc* problems in the chain before they absorb further resources and detrimentally affect the bottom line.

SOURCES OF HIGH MARKETING COST

Multicountry studies show how revealing such analysis can be in identifying the real cost of servicing each segment, distribution channel and product group. ABC dispenses with the misguided evidence based on traditional cost analysis and places more emphasis on what is actually happening in the field. It also provides the basis for monitoring the operational implications arising from the changing market and product conditions, provoking incremental complexity and, ultimately, the higher costs it imposes on the marketing units.

In particular, the ABC technique should draw more attention to the costs of sustaining the customers' business. These are traceable to individual customers and reveal the real costs to serve them, which may be totally independent of sales volume. They cover a myriad of activities such as calls on customers (travel, entertainment, order-taking paper based transactions, etc), and the back-room activities back at HQ in developing and maintaining background information on each customer's operations.

The true cost of sustaining business in various customer segments might reveal any of the following unacceptable cost factors associated with customer-related tasks:

- extensive customer-sustaining activities (special promotions, customer-site calls, travel, data collection and retention, etc)
- special or over-elaborate packaging
- complex invoicing
- dispersed and frequent deliveries of small lots
- routine customer inquiries or complaints answering effort
- inordinately time-consuming customers
- onerous accounts receivable effort
- delays in processing transactions
- support activities and inefficiencies in providing these internal services.

Table 4.8 shows some guidelines in building a revised accounting system associated with marketing activities.

Table 4.8 *The revised accounting system*

All costs must be allocated to those activities that generated these charges

The list of marketing-related activities to be controlled should be limited to only the big marketing and support expenditure items to prevent miscoding, obsessive accuracy or a disproportionate administrative effort

Activity costs should be allocated to particular products or marketing units

Common overheads incurred on behalf of all products or business units should not, however, be apportioned to products or business units

The allocation system should take account of activities that transcend unit and functional boundaries; this makes more sense in analysing costs compared to the traditional segregation of costs by cost centres, and business units

Costs should be allocated and coded to activities as an integral part of accounting procedures; this guarantees that activity cost data is timely and avoids having to re-key the data after it has been posted to the accounting records

REVISED RELATIONSHIP WITH HIGH-VOLUME CLIENTS

Some companies discovered that the ABC exercise threw a different light on relationships with large sales-volume customers, such
as hypermarket store groups, previously believed to be the most
profitable. The economic value of handling large-volume orders
placed by giant retail buying groups, was found to be less lucrative when the services required of them were examined more
closely: concessions were expected from suppliers in the form of
lower prices, returned goods not sold within the month, longer
settlement periods, frequent deliveries of small volumes, extensive sales and technical assistance, product modifications and tactical in-store promotional support, etc. Knowledge of the costs-to-
serve particular customers or distribution channels could enable
marketing heads to modify the way they do business with these
retail groups, and provide the basis of a more informed dialogue
with them on all aspects of the business relationship.

Enhanced economic value can be introduced through price
adjustments, minimum orders or exercising greater selectivity in
terms of orders accepted. In addition, the components of each
marketing activity cost pool can be reviewed to trim any unnecessary tasks, which are not essential for meeting the customers'
demands – ie excessive paperwork, extensive sales calls to stores,
frequent price changes, etc.

The key question guiding the cost-control policy resides in monitoring which parts of the organization are expanding as it increases the diversity of its product lines, its customer base and its distribution channels. Insights into cost components can be used to
provide a rational basis for better budget-setting associated with
overhead costs in response to changes in the activity mix of the
organization. Little progress will be gained in understanding the
cost behaviour if overhead costs are arbitrarily allocated to constantly growing and changing product lines. While senior management may not be able to manage costs, it can now improve its
knowledge of the different components of marketing activity,
which consume costs

WHAT NEXT?

Once the real costs of each customer-related activity are made 'visible' as a result of an ABC exercise, senior management can envisage treating them as cost centres. This will imply four steps.

■ Identifying all functions and tasks related to customer support throughout the organization
■ Examining how they function. What value do they add ? Do customers perceive them as adding value ?
■ Treating the activities as cost centres and managing them as an integral part of the customer life-cycle.
■ Identifying unnecessary tasks, and thus costs, associated with this cycle – those activities and processes that add a cost but no value.

THE STRATEGIC IMPLICATIONS

ABC will help marketing management to optimize profitability by reinforcing the culture that improved profitability depends primarily on whether and to what extent customer-specific costs are recovered in the net profits. Two central actions could be envisaged to improve profits. The first is in adjusting the pricing policy: those products that make onerous demands on support services and on sales staff should bear a higher price tag; high-volume products that have tended to subsidize the others should benefit from lower prices. A complete review of the product mix could be taken to achieve a level of lower demands on resources or augment sales revenue for the same consumption of resources.

The second action, and critically perhaps more important, is to identify ways to reduce resource consumption. This could consist of streamlining processes, using IT more intelligently to centralize customer orders and their processing, and reorganizing delivery schedules. Simply cutting costs will not be enough: the freed-up resources should either be re-deployed elsewhere or cut and reflected in a revised budget proposal. Failure to take this action will create excess capacity but not increase profits.

A range of activities associated with each customer or distributor need to be studied in detail, to elucidate the absolute and incremental costs linked with production and distribution of each product from beginning to the end of the value chain. Even small-scale improvements to processes, if multiplied a dozen times, lead to cost savings. One US hotel chain uncovered unexpected costs associated with different services – cleaning activities for executive suites vs regular rooms – but this was not reflected in the rates charged. Examples of business processes that can become complex and costly include:

- ordering customers' products
- small order sizes
- manual processing
- significant amounts of pre- and post-sales support
- requirement for specialized inventories
- slow payments.

The bottom line is the necessity to eliminate non-customer-valued activities through, for example, the re-design of delivery systems, the restructuring of the accounts collection activity or the streamlining of multiple in-house quality checks. Marketing staff might consider putting on less special promotions for, and sales staff might pay less routine calls on, those customer groups whose business is not profitable when all costs are taken into account. The ABC methodology should not, however, be used by senior managers to indiscriminately eliminate products, drop customers or outsource certain non-core activities. The outcome should guide them in reviewing the company's marketing policy, modifying the customer and/or product mix, or in finding more productive means of performing activities and customer transactions.

CALCULATING THE COST OF THE CUSTOMER VALUE-CHAIN

Delivering customer satisfaction is not limited to the marketing and sales functions; various other functions may be partially involved in the process – customer service, logistics, finance and so on. Grasping the total costs associated with a typical order-cycle requires tracing the sequential steps in the customer-fulfilment process, all the way from sales planning to the ultimate delivery of goods to the customer. Consider a simplified example below of fulfilling an order for a major-volume customer. This involves five items.

- Identifying which units in the organization are involved – marketing (planning and organization), sales (order-seeking/taking), customer services (order-processing/logistics) and finance (cost estimates/pricing and billing).
- Estimating the approximate time taken to accomplish each task or sub-task in fulfilling the order.
- Working out the direct costs of salaries of the staff involved.
- Calculating the proportionate cost of accomplishing the task or sub-task – ie annual salary of the staff person working on the task and the approximate time spent on the specific task or sub-task like billing:
- A finance/accounting assistant staff's salary = FF130,000 pa x 60 per cent pa of time employed in conducting the billing task = FF78,000 pa.
- Calculating the aggregate cost of accomplishing all these tasks and sub-tasks by adding up the proportionate costs involved.

In the example in Table 4.9, assume that the annual salaries are of the following magnitude:

Marketing manager	FF350,000
Sales representative	FF180,000
Customer services assistant	FF120,000
Finance/accounting assistant	FF130,000

Table 4.9 *Proportionate cost of order-fulfilment for Customer A*

Resources	% cost Marketing unit	% cost Sales unit	% cost Customer services	% cost Finance unit	Total cost
	(1 staff person)	(2 staff persons)	(1 staff person)	(1 staff person)	
Tasks					
Sales planning	20% 70,000				70,000
Order-seeking		30% 108,000			108,000
Order-cost	5%		35%	10%	72,500

estimates and negotiation of delivery dates	17,500		42,000	13,000	
Order-taking and receipt	2% 7,000	25% 90,000			97,000
Order-processing			40% 48,000		48,000
Order-delivery			10% 12,000		12,000
Invoices prepared and despatched				60% 78,000	78,000
Installation difficulties or errors in orders (1)		7% 12,600	12% 14,400		27,000
Order rectified (1)		3% 5,400	10% 12,000	4% 5,200	22,600
Total cost	94,500	216,000	128,400	96,200	535,100

(1) Assume one staff person

Senior management now has a broad picture of what it costs the organization to fulfil an order with this customer, when all the tasks and sub-tasks have been identified and measured in terms of the proportionate cost of the staff salary. The aggregate cost of this activity is FF535,100. Four questions should now be addressed.

- Should the order be accepted, given the total direct costs involved?
- Can certain tasks or sub-tasks be minimized, simplified, automated, eliminated, etc in order to reduce the resources deployed in conducting them?
- Could non-customer activities – ie tasks that have no direct link with the customer *per se*, like billing, planning, processing etc – be outsourced to reduce costs?
- Assuming a recurrent level of installation problems or delivery errors, can such after-sales occurrences be reduced to avoid additional costs within the customer-services and finance

units, responsible for rectifying the orders? Can after-sales activities be outsourced to less expensive tele-marketing firms with mobile staff to intervene when problems occur?

A multitude of structural issues and questions can emerge from this analysis, providing senior management with the means to identify costly activities in the long chain of events associated with customer order-processing fulfilment. More importantly, cost data now provides a basis for judging whether orders should be accepted given their complexity and incremental costs, and staff effort re-deployed to real customer-related issues rather than paper-processing.

KEY ISSUES

■ Marketing costs are inherently difficult to manage at micro- (marketing department) or macro- (corporate HQ) organizational level. They tend to be too aggregated, discretionary and dispersed to be managed on a sustainable basis. But while costs may be difficult to manage, activities are not!

■ Differentiated marketing policies – multiple brands selling across multiple market segments with tactically different promotional campaigns – have made the task of tracking costs, revenues and the profit streams, associated with individual products much more complex.

■ The use of direct labour or percentage of sales as an allocation basis for measuring marketing expenditure, is inadequate: worse again, it may be misleading.

■ Spreading the fixed costs over a larger number of customer bases make the figures look better; but they conceal the real costs-to-serve each product, distribution channel and market segment, customer group and distribution outlet.

■ A costing system must mirror the entire marketing operation, transcending different functional departments, tracing the time and complexity associated with each market segment.

■ Activity Based Costing (ABC) strives to track the costs of the diverse marketing operation by (1) considering all costs as product expenses, and (2) segregating activities, and thus costs, to individual products.

■ ABC also offers an opportunity to identify unnecessary tasks, reporting systems, transactions, processing operations, etc that simply do not add value in terms of quality, use appearance or customer features.

- The key question is: 'Which parts of the organization tend to grow as the company increases the diversity of its product line, its customer base and its marketing channels?' The marketing support activities associated with contemporary marketing are growing exponentially, but is the costing system sufficiently synchronized with these developments?
- ABC should be an ongoing measure of marketing performance: which market, product, distribution channel is using what corporate resources?
- The company needs to identify the high – and sometimes hidden – sources of marketing cost corresponding to each product, market or distribution channel, such as sustaining customer business.
- Improved profitability depends on whether and to what extent the customer-specific costs are recovered in the net profits.

[1] Adapted from a case by R Maynard/Management Accounting (December 1995)

BIBLIOGRAPHY

AMA Industry Forum, 'Cutting expenses: cost management is the key' (October 1992)

A Anandarajan and H Joseph Wen, 'Ensuring cost effectiveness in implementing client/server systems: an activity-based approach', *Management Accounting* (November 1997)

D Bohl, 'Do we need a new alphabet for cost management?', *AMA Executive Management Forum* (April 1991)

K Cleland, 'The flip side of ABC... contribution-based activity', *Management Accounting* (May 1997)

R Cooper, 'You need a new cost system when...', *Harvard Business Review* (January-February 1989)

R Cooper and R Kaplan, 'Measure costs right: make the right decisions', *Harvard Business Review* (September-October 1988)

R Cooper and R Kaplan, 'Profit priorities from activity-based costing', *Harvard Business Review* (May-June 1991)

T Dickson, 'The power tools of a DIY strategy', *Financial Times* (August 1995)

The Economist, 'Costing the factory of the future' (2 March 1990)

G Foster and M Gupta, 'Marketing cost management and management accounting', *Journal of Management Accounting Research* (Fall 1994)

I Hamilton-Fazey, 'Learning the lesson of ABC', *Financial Times* (6 April 1992)

R Henkoff, 'Cost cutting: how to do it right so you don't have to do it again', *Fortune* (9 April 1990)

H T Johnson and R Kaplan, 'Relevance Lost: the rise and fall of management accounting', *Harvard Business School Press* (1987)

A Kennedy, 'ABC basics', *Management Accounting* (June 1996)

R Lewis, 'Activity-based costing for marketing', *Management Accounting* (USA) (November 1991)

M Lucas, 'Absorption costing for decision-making', *Management Accounting* (October 1997)

R Maynard, 'Business processing accounting', *Management Accounting* (December 1995)

D Osborne and N Ringrose, 'Market-focused cost reduction', *Management Accounting* (January 1998)

K Pennary, 'The productivity paradox', *International Business Week* (6 June 1988)

T Pryor, 'It's time to throw away cost accounting Ten Commandments', *AMA Finance Forum* (July 1990)

C Sevin, 'Analyzing your cost of marketing', *Small Business Administration* (April 1973)

D Waller, 'How to bring technology to account', *Financial Times* (21 January 1991)

5

OPTIMIZING THE MARKETING COST AND REVENUE RELATIONSHIP

OBSESSION WITH SALES VOLUME

Many companies still measure their marketing performance with techniques developed in conditions that were appropriate in the past. Sales volume, or revenue, targets continue to be the ommipresent performance measurement. Meanwhile, a myriad of sales activities are pursued at a cost level that is frequently disproportionate to the ultimate value of the earnings, and fails to be measured. This problem is compounded by the lack of appropriate information within the marketing operation about working capital employed and the impact of marketing decisions on the cash position of the organization.

It has long been assumed that since most marketing expenditure is of a discretionary nature, control could be exercised through traditional variance analysis. This approach imposes on the marketing department the routine tasks of (1) analysing actual expenses from budget, (2) explaining those variances and the corrective action to be envisaged and (3) readjusting the forecasts for remainder of the year.

The problem is that variances in marketing expenses serve to indicate only whether more or less funds have been spent than originally budgeted. While variance analysis is important to understand what is happening at expenditure level, it fails to tell marketing heads anything about the efficiency of its activities. Limited attempts are made to segregate discretionary expenses and the working capital used by the individual products, with a view to devolving responsibility to product managers in order to optimize performance of these items. This results in senior management constantly trying to find the right balance within the company to avoid indiscriminate cut-backs in marketing development costs to compensate for unfavourable manufacturing cost variances; typically, just before the end of year, and in response to outside shareholder pressure for profitable results, the marketing budget gets clawed back to ensure the attainment of the short-term profit objectives.

More importantly, variance analysis reveals little about the effectiveness of marketing effort. While the efficiency of marketing efforts can be monitored with the help of this analysis by asking the pertinent question: 'Are we doing things right?', the measurement of effectiveness in the form of 'Are we doing the right things?' remains elusive. Such notions are difficult to measure if the corporate reporting system relies exclusively on sales volume or revenue concerns. Deeper questioning of each new and current activity within the marketing department is required to measure the cost and revenue streams of each. The development of a new sales planning system, illustrated in Table 5.1, underlines the importance of distinguishing between the two notions and the value of getting the balance right: is all of the energy and attention paid by the marketing people to 'do things right' overwhelming the time devoted to 'doing the right things', like satisfying the client?

Improvements in efficiency and effectiveness associated with the marketing activity will remain elusive as long as the cost and revenue relationship ignored.

Yet these problems go to the heart of improved returns on marketing expenditure. Key strategic marketing decisions increasingly involve heavy investments in the intangible sources of potential competitive advantage such as brands and customer relationships. These expenditures are much more vague and nebulous for financial management than production operations, where various financial models exist to guide the choice of whether to proceed with business investments. Such reasoning explains perhaps why less rigorous financial reviews are used by financial management in taking a closer look at marketing expenses.

For major tangible investments, finance managers call upon conventional models of net present value (NPV) and discounted cash flow (DCF) calculations to decide whether, for instance, to invest in a factory: this would start with the calculation of the project's NPV – that is, an estimate of future cash flows, discounted to today's value, which are then compared with the result to the original cost of the investment. If the result is positive, senior management would go ahead with the project, provided it met the criteria on investment.

Table 5.1 *Measuring the effectiveness and efficiency of marketing effort*

Concepts	Description	Characteristics	Measurement	Example: New sales planning system
Efficiency	Are we doing things right?	Easy to observe and measure against standards but not always indicative of the bottom line	Activity level Costs Key ratios and indicators	May save sales staff 1 hour per day
Effectiveness	Are we doing the right things?	Indirect, subjective evaluation normally affects profit	Revenue Market share Competitive perception	Impact in real terms if sales staff spend time freed-up in pursuit of other productive ends – ie customer-related activities

Source: Doyle, Strategic Management (1990).

LACK OF COST AND REVENUE INFORMATION

Part of the problem in measuring marketing effectiveness is that marketing people have no real knowledge of the investments (costs) required throughout the organization to improve revenues. Equally, important working capital elements like stocks and accounts receivable are not part of the marketing function's responsibilities. This prevents them from managing another important measure of effectiveness – future cashflows arising from sales. Sales volume alone is an inadequate measure of success or failure in many marketing environments.

The problem is not resolved by simply attributing a revenue-centre status to marketing units. In a revenue centre, outputs are measured in monetary terms but no attempt is made to relate the inputs (ie expenses or costs) to outputs. If expenses were matched with revenues, the marketing activity could be better assessed as a profit centre. But few marketing departments have profit responsibilities. Actual sales or orders reserved are measured against budgets. No account is taken of the 'expense' nature of the marketing activities because the revenue centres are not charged for the cost of goods that they market. The net result is that the manager of a typical marketing revenue-generating centre does not have knowledge of the elements that are needed to make the cost/revenue trade-off required for optimum marketing decisions.

FINANCIAL CONTROL CONCERNS

The implications for financial controls are fundamentally different in managing marketing costs. At best, activities can be divided into 'order-getting' and 'order-fulfilment': the first category involves test marketing, selling activities, advertising and sales promotion. While the output can be measured, the effectiveness of the marketing effort is difficult to evaluate because the environment in which the company operates is not always controllable. The order-fulfilment activities are more transparent and can be subject to more objective assessment. These activities comprise processing the orders, transportation of goods to distribution centres, warehousing, logistics and delivery costs, sales staff salaries and commissions, invoicing and collecting amounts due by the customers. While the responsibility centres that perform these tasks will transcend different units within the organization the expenses represent largely engineered costs that can be controlled through standard costs and budgets and benchmarked against best performers in the industry.

SELLING EXPENSES IGNORED

Even if an attempt is made to allocate reasonably accurate costs to marketing units for control purposes, adhering to budget targets for selling expenses is rarely a major part of the evaluation of marketing performance. If a product group sells significantly above its targets, senior management is not likely to be concerned if it exceeds its budgeted cost by 15 per cent. The sheer impact of sales volume on the bottom line is so important that it tends to obscure the cost performance. This explains why few corporations assess a marketing operation primarily on its ability to match its cost targets, let alone attempt to control the costs of the activity. Again, the sales target remains the key factor in the evaluation process.

The control thrust inherent in monitoring order-fulfilment activities is not always appropriate for order-getting activities. Lack of appreciation of this detail can lead to wrong decisions. If, for example, a reasonably positive correlation can be established between sales volume and the degree of sales promotion and advertising investments, it would be fallacious to assume that sales expenses are a variable element – ie they are costs that changes in total in proportion to changes in sales volume. Budgets that are adjusted to changes in sales volume will not help in controlling selling expenses. Adjustments to sales promotion and advertising expenses to respond to short-term changes in sales volume do not always make sense, either. Companies, however, continue to set marketing expense budgets as a percentage of budgeted sales, on the assumption that the higher the sales volumes, the more the company can afford to invest in advertising.

Another feature ignored in the control process are the sales rebates and other inducements to encourage the trade and/or customers to buy, which are not measured in terms of their likely impact on cashflows.

DEVELOPING A PROFIT-CENTRE APPROACH

One way of providing a greater focus over expense and revenue items associated with marketing operations is to develop a profit-centre structure for each major marketing functional unit. The marketing department can then be transformed into brand or product groupings who 'buy' services from other parts of the organization, and who can 'sell' to outside clients in the full knowledge of the costs involved and the revenue potential of each customer group: the outcome can be judged only in terms of a profit, not just sales volume. Management decisions involving increased expenditures are thus made in the expectation of enhanced sales revenue. Such decisions would be taken in the context of expense/revenue trade-offs. Would increased sales outlets or additional customer-service personnel to handle inquiries and installation problems result in increased sales revenue? Implementing such delegated authority, however, requires that two conditions exist:

- the marketing unit must have the relevant information in making cost/revenue trade-offs
- there should be some objective means of measuring how effectively the marketing unit manager is making such trade-offs.

With regard to the first concern, the marketing unit needs a degree of control over three broad types of decision.

- The product decision: what products or services should the marketing unit sell?
- The sourcing decision: on what basis should the products be obtained – ie manufactured in-house or bought outside?
- The marketing decision: what sales techniques and media should be used, and at what price should they be offered in each market?

While the manager of the marketing unit may have limited control over the entire range of business functions, the decision to become a profit centre should be taken when the marketing unit exercises enough influence over the activities that affect the unit's profitability. The marketing activity would be charged with the cost of products sold. Significant levels of in-house services such as customer billing, packaging, transport, legal advice, staff training, IT services, etc can also be charged to this unit, rendering it a semi-autonomous entity, capable of deciding what products and corporate services it requires, and at what price.

A transfer price – the price one in-house unit charges for a service, or a product supplied to the marketing unit – provides it with the relevant information to make the optimum revenue/cost trade-offs. The transfer price creates revenue for the 'selling' (manufacturing) sub-unit and a purchase cost for the 'buying' (marketing) unit, affecting operating income numbers for both units. The operating incomes can then be used to evaluate the performance of each sub-unit and to motivate managers to take decisions that will maximize the spread between costs and revenues of conducting their business.

The marketing 'buying' unit manager, for example, should be charged, by the manufacturing 'selling' unit for the product range on the basis of a standard cost transfer price, not the actual cost of the product sold. This allows for a separation of manufacturing cost performance from the marketing performance. Since the marketing manager has no control over the way the manufacturing unit is run, he is not penalized by inefficiencies associated with the manufacturing operation.

Considerable advantages can accrue from such an approach.

Improved control over diverse marketing operations

The profit-centre approach becomes more relevant – and creates greater transparency between cost and revenues and their optimum relationship – the more diverse the marketing operation becomes – ie multiple products selling in multiple markets. Centralized control over key decisions of a local nature are placed on the shoulders of those better placed to judge the situation: the marketing units. Answers to specific marketing questions can be more readily weighed: What marketing techniques should be used? What should be spent on advertising and sales promotion? How should it be spent, and in which media? Should existing sales staff or local agents be used? Which market segments should be targeted?

Better sourcing decisions

The profit-centre marketing manager should be able to put together a product for a given market that is more competitive and much faster than a fully integrated company. On the revenue side, the decentralization associated with the profit-centre structure also allows the local management to inject life into brands and make them relevant to local customers.

The 'selling' profit centre (manufacturing) will also benefit from this approach. With excess global capacity in almost every product sector, pricing pressures are increasing. One possible way of meeting these pressures is to pursue a scale strategy – spreading costs and revenues across the world. Operating on a global scale means having the full cost information associated with the sourcing and marketing of the company's products. The fundamentals of the business may also need to be called into question, and outsourcing certain parts or all of the manufacturing function may be necessary. From a global corporate perspective, benchmarking production costs with outside players should also lead to an understanding as to why the outside costs are lower.

Increased flexibility

The principal motivating factor for the marketing unit manager is the freedom to source his products outside if the price is more competitive. Equally, he or she should be able to 'buy in' service provision for such items as transport, packaging, billing and after-sales service, if over a sustainable period of time it can be proven that the rates are lower. Reduced complexity and lower administrative costs may also be an incentive for the marketing unit, concerned with freeing-up its own staff time to deal with the customer rather than processing paperwork resulting from increased levels of sales activity. In this instance, the only appropriate transfer price policy should be one that gives the marketing manager the right to deal with either insider or outsiders, at their discretion, based on the most competitive rate over the long run. The 'market' thus establishes the transfer price. The decision to manufacture inside or rely on in-house services (legal affairs, billing, quality control, MIS, etc) or go outside for these 'services and products', will depend on what the marketplace is prepared to pay. In theory, this would signify that if the marketing unit cannot get a satisfactory rate from an inside source for a specific product or service, they should be free to buy from an outside source.

ESTABLISHING A TRANSFER PRICE

Clearly, a method has to be found to agree on a transfer price, which is both simple and transparent to all parties and empowers them to optimize results of their units. There are three broad methods for determining transfer prices.

- Market-based transfer price – the choice of a price of a similar product or service based on prevailing rates in external markets – ie those used by the 'best player' in the market.
- Cost-based prices – the choice of a price based on manufacturing the product in question. This can take the form of fixed and variable manufacturing costs, with a portion of administrative cost included in the price. The tendency is to use either a standard full cost rather than actual costs, for the reasons explained above, or full costs plus a mark-up.
- Negotiated transfer price – where the sub-units are free to negotiate the transfer prices between themselves and then decide whether to buy and sell internally or deal with outside entities. These prices can be used when constant change occurs in the marketplace.

Ultimately, the appropriate transfer price method should result in each unit manager making the optimal decisions for the organization as a whole. In particular, it should promote corporate goal congruence focused on a sustained high level of marketing effort aimed at satisfying the customer – at a profit – over the long term. Congruence can be achieved by providing the cost and revenue information to inspire sellers, buyers and the whole organization.

- Sellers (the internal manufacturing or corporate support service unit) to provide a product or service at the most competitive price by holding down the costs and rationalizing and automating when necessary.
- Buyers (the marketing unit) to acquire and use the inputs efficiently, fully possessing a knowledge (1) of the cost structure, (2) the maximum price 'ceiling' the customer is prepared to pay and (3) the potential volume the market can handle at any one time.
- The whole organization should be motivated to pursue a continuous value analysis reviewing manufacturing methods, pricing strategy, tactical marketing campaigns, product ranges, etc.

Intra-company transactions signify that the buying and selling units must deal with each other at 'arm's length' and that the transfer prices approximate the rates operative as if the profit centres were independent companies. There can be considerable problems, however, in integrated companies, where the marketing units may not even be aware of the amount of upstream fixed cost and 'profit margin' in its internal purchase price. Consider the following example:

Unit A (manufacturing) sells 1,000 items of product to Unit B (marketing) for £35, comprising:

	£
Variable cost	5
Fixed cost	20
Profit	10
Price	35

In this example, the transfer price of £35 per product is a variable cost as far as the marketing unit is concerned. However, the company's variable cost for this product is £5. The marketing unit does not have the right information to make appropriate short-term marketing decisions; the transfer price system obscures the relevant costs to the marketing unit and if they knew the company's variable costs, business could be taken at a lower price under specific conditions. The alternative approach might consist of covering fixed costs with longer-term contracts, which ignores the variable cost and profit element.

The problem can be addressed by using a two-part price for transfers between units, consisting of (1) a charge equal to a standard variable cost of production; and (2) a total monthly charge equal to the fixed costs associated with the facilities reserved for the marketing unit. Returning to our example, unit A (manufacturing unit) would reserve a capacity to produce 1,000 items of the product per year for Unit B (marketing); the standard variable cost per item is established at £5. The fixed costs per month are calculated as being £20,000 and the investment required (essentially, working capital – inventory, accounts receivable, and fixed-asset components) to produce 1,000 items of £10,000. The revised transfer price for each product sold by Unit A to Unit B would be:

Variable cost	£5 x 1,000 = 5,000
Monthly fixed cost + profit	= 30,000 (20,000 + 10,000)
Price	£35,000
or £35 per unit	

This is the same price as under the single method above. If transfers in another month were less than 1,000 items – for example, 800 items – the price structure would be:

Variable cost   £5 x 800 = 4,000
Monthly fixed
cost + profit   = 30,000 (20,000 + 10,000)
Price   £34,000/800
= £42.5 per unit

The differential of £7.50 paid by the marketing unit is a penalty for not using the capacity reserved by Unit A. However, the marketing unit would gain in another month by using this two-step method if the capacity ordered was higher, ie 1,200 items

Variable cost   £5 x 1,200 = £6,000
FC+ profit   £30,000 = £30,000
                 = £36,000/1,200
                 = £30

The differential of £5 represents the economies that the manufacturing unit would generate because it could produce additional items without entailing additional fixed costs.

Because the variable cost to the marketing unit is the same as that of the company as a whole, the company's profit is consequently optimized by optimizing the unit's profit. The marketing unit should now be able to make appropriate short-term marketing decisions. In the wider context, the marketing unit also has detailed information about the upstream fixed costs and profit relating to the product, which can be used to make improved marketing decisions in the longer-term.

To improve its transfer price, the marketing unit could negotiate periodically with the manufacturing unit regarding the monthly charges for fixed costs and profit, which would depend on the capacity reserved for them; sales forecasting will obviously need to be more realistic. The intra-company pricing system will raise some problems, not least the accuracy in determining the fixed cost and investment allocation. Most companies have little difficulty in allocating costs and assets (both fixed and current) to individual products. It is important to avoid excessive and time-consuming calculations; approximate calculations are sufficient. The key impediment is in determining the capacity to be dedicated to produce a particular product. Generally, if capacity is earmarked for multiple products sold to the same marketing unit, there may be no necessity to allocate fixed costs and investments to individual products of the unit.

MAKING THE MARKETING DEPARTMENT MORE ACCOUNTABLE

The overall goal of the intra-company transfer price, linked to the profit-centre structure, is in providing the marketing people, who ultimately sell to the outside customer, with the appropriate information and motivation to (1) gain a greater awareness of the costs associated with the product and matching it with the revenue streams, (2) be more selective in accepting certain orders given the costs and constraints they have to work with, (3) consider different sourcing options, (4) keep down the fixed cost nature of the company's activities, and (5) maximize company profits.

Of course, a profit-centre structure does not assume that marketing units will be capable of controlling everything; very few expense items are entirely controllable by them but they can exert some influence over those running the 'selling' units. In order to provide a performance measurement mechanism that is both fair and manageable, marketing unit managers could be held responsible for the following areas:

- all profit and loss items generated by the marketing profit centre
- any expense incurred outside the marketing profit centre at corporate headquarters or in other units, for which they can be invoiced
- a corporate expense item comprising controllable working capital – ie accounts receivable and inventory, multiplied by an interest rate representing the cost of capital, for instance.

Such a charge is required to take account of trade-offs between the levels of working capital and profits. It is conceivable that under these conditions, high levels of inventory can reduce lost business due to inadequate stocks. Equally, a more flexible policy on credit terms may result in higher sales. In the final analysis, only the marketing profit-centre head understands and can exploit these trade-offs. If working capital budget targets are neither appropriate or feasible, an interest charge would represent an incentive for the marketing head to make these trade-offs to optimize the company's profits. By demonstrating that profits can be increased beyond the costs of carrying inventories and accounts receivable, the whole company benefits.

MEASURING PROFITABILITY OF THE MARKETING UNIT

Another consideration is a mechanism to measure how effectively the marketing unit is managing the cost/revenue trade-offs. It is clear that marketing unit managers should be measured only against those items they can influence. In a typical company, these will probably be all expenses incurred directly by that unit – ie cost of sales and perhaps some variable costs. For example, consider the following contribution margin profiles:

	$
Revenue	2,000
Cost of sales	600
Gross margin	1,400
Variable costs	200
Contribution	1,200

The main attraction of using the contribution margin to maximize the marketing unit's performance is its simplicity. It supports the assumption the marketing unit cannot control the fixed expenses incurred elsewhere – even if it is made on its behalf. The focus becomes one of maximizing the spread between revenue and variable expenses.

But this assumption fails to take account of the significant lumps of fixed cost capacity and support service input deployed by central HQ or other profit centres on behalf of the marketing unit. Real profit will only emerge when all the relevant costs associated with that unit are absorbed by adequate revenues. Consideration should be given to re-allocating other marketing charges incurred elsewhere in the organization:

	$
Contribution	1,200
(1) Other marketing unit costs	130
(2) Charges from other corporate centres incurred for the Marketing unit	60
	190
Direct marketing unit profit	1,010

This measures the amount of corporate overhead that the marketing unit absorbs. It covers two categories of expenses, (1) those incurred directly in the marketing unit, ie sales promotion, direct mailing advertising, packaging, graphics, travel, etc and (2) all charges that can be identified as having been spent on behalf of this unit by other cost and/or profit centres (ie postal charges, IT material, rental charges, etc). The marketing department now has to absorb these expenses and should be more vigilant in ensuring value for money in the use of these services. This is facilitated by having a greater say in deciding how much of these services they wish to use.

RESIDUAL CORPORATE EXPENSES

Certain residual expenses (3) incurred by central head office could also be re-allocated to the marketing unit:

	$
Marketing unit profit	1,010
(3) Other corporate expenses	30
Marketing unit profit	980

This represents common charges incurred by HQ for the whole organization and not directly related to the marketing unit *per se*. But the marketing unit can still exert some influence over the efficiency in delivering services such as accounts receivable, maintenance and upkeep of machinery and buildings, IT services, or R & D. Improved cost transparency should lead to pressure by the marketing people to reduce the amount of support input they request from other parts of the company. It should also result in calls for improved productivity for support services provided to all parts of the organization, especially now that the marketing unit is being billed for these corporate expenses.

MANAGING THE CASH POSITION

The most visible performance gauge of the marketing units efforts will be the ability to generate positive cash flows. Any effort to increase the sales effort will involve cash. Generating profitable business produces cash. The problem is that cash usually flows out more quickly before it flows in, especially when the business is growing fast. Unless sales and buying transactions can be matched, excess cash outflows over a lengthy period forces the company to raise additional cash through loans or equity offerings. The marketing function has a key role to play in contributing to better cash management.

Revenue increases of 50-100 per cent a year, due to the launch of a new product or an improved distribution, may be an indication of marketing efficiency. This may also improve the profits, but it is not guaranteed. Little, if anything, is known by the marketing people about how increased sales activities can influence the cash position of the organization, frequently leading to projects being stalled. Marketing activities aimed at increasing sales tend to provoke the following actions:

- releasing cash to buy or build fixed assets through the capital budgeting process
- stepping up purchases, thereby increasing both raw materials, stocks and accounts payable
- an eventual build-up of finished goods stock
- increased investments in accounts receivable, bad debts, etc.

All of these actions will have occurred before any new cash has been generated from the marketplace. Even when the expected sales do occur, they will still lag behind the generation of cash until the customer pays. Eventual late payments by customers will stretch the company's cash situation even further.

Measuring this aspect of the new marketing profit centres' responsibility is required. In particular, the marketing unit centre has to plan for growth in its activities within the limits of normal working capital sources, without the need for external injections of finance. Increasingly, the marketing unit has to manage the cash implications of its activities and evolve towards for self-financiable growth by productively deploying assets, liabilities and capital. The cash situation can be managed on the basis of a product or product line, a market segment or a distribution channel. Some units can survive with apparently high liabilities because they have time to pay and can generate cash quickly. This is the example of many retail groups who demand 90 days' credit from its suppliers, but offer no credit at all to its customers. The key elements to manage are the cash tied up in stock, accounts receivable and accounts payable, encapsulated in the notion of working capital:

Working capital = Stock + Accounts receivable – Accounts payable

The aim is to maintain a reasonable balance between these variables. But what is this minimum level? How is it calculated? The marketing unit may rightly argue that retaining a depleted level of working capital will adversely affect sales, thus profits, because:

- a stock-out or inadequate stock level could lead to customers not having a wide enough choice and going elsewhere, and thus lost business
- strict credit terms or no credit may result in disaffection of customers
- by offering no credit facilities to suppliers, they may no longer wish to source the unit.

There are clearly established links between profitability and cash: if a business unit wants to increase profitability, it requires extra working capital. But there is a world of difference between profits announced by the company and the cash it generates! One of Europe's leading telecommunications equipment manufacturers discovered that in spite of 20 consecutive quarters of improved order bookings, its cashflow, before financial activities, was negative. This resulted from strong growth driven by larger stock and increased vendor finance. The telecom equipment supplier was increasingly providing support to operators in the form of either finance or consultancy, as a way of opening markets. Such added-on services adversely affected the cashflow situation, even if the ultimate result was expected to be profitable.

In reality, the working capital needed to finance increased growth is dependent on the organization's own resources. Consider the simplified structure of the Balance Sheet in Figure 5.2: it shows two distinct categories of accounts, the upper half (stock + accounts receivable – accounts payable) which represents the need for working capital. This reflects the real need for cash by the organization to generate sales growth. Stock purchased to manufacture the goods, value of goods sold but not yet paid, less the supplier's debt, is the amount of cash outstanding that the company needs to finance. The lower half (long-term debt + stock holders' equity – fixed assets) represents the base of working capital, or the internal resources. A balance has been maintained between both equations.

Stock	200	Accounts payable	200
Accounts receivable	300	Taxes payable	50
		Long-term debt	350
		Capital	250
Fixed Assets	500	Retained earnings (Profit)	150

Stock + A/c rec. – A/c pay + taxes pay
200 + 300 – 250 = 250
Debt + Capital + Profits – Fixed assets
350 + 250 + 150 – 500 = 500

Now consider a growing company in Figure 5.3, showing larger blocks of working capital compared to needs for working capital. This represents a situation in which the base of available internal resources is sufficient to self-finance the needs of working capital, thus generating a cash positive situation.

Stock	200	Accounts payable	200
Accounts receivable	250	Taxes payable	50
CASH	+50	Long-term debt	300
		Capital	400
Fixed Assets	500	Retained earnings (Profit)	50

Stock + A/c rec. – A/c pay + taxes pay
200 + 250 – 250 = 200
Debt + Capital + Profits – Fixed assets
300 + 400 + 50 – 500= 250
Difference = 50 (surplus)

In another scenario ambitious plans to expand sales could result in a situation where the need for working capital exceeds the working capital base, as shown in Figure 5.3, generating a negative cash result.

Stock	350	Accounts payable	200
Accounts receivable	250	Taxes payable	50
Fixed assets	500	CASH	–100
		Long-term debt	300
		Capital	400
		Retained earnings (Profit)	50

Stock + A/c rec. – A/c pay + taxes payable
350 + 250 – 250 = 350
Debt + Capital + Profits – Fixed assets
300 + 400 + 50 – 500= 250
Difference = (100)

These three scenarios demonstrate the importance of cash management. Marketing units that pursue increased levels of sales activity trigger off a build-up in stocks (raw materials, work-in-progress and finished goods 'in stock') and a growth of sales orders (sales on credit); this evolves to a situation where cash is 'immobilized' in the business. Cash arising from sales orders is not available to the business until everything is sold and paid for. Amounts which are owed to suppliers actually represent cash not yet disbursed and thus retained in the business until the payment date fixed with the supplier; the difference between both amounts is the outstanding cash position to be financed (need for working capital).

The counter-balancing amounts, representing the available base of cash to finance the growing business (debt + capital + profits), which also could include profits carried forward from previous periods, should be sufficient to match the outstanding cash.

An improved cash management culture within the marketing unit can be promoted by developing and implementing clear and simple cashflow guidelines for all the staff to follow. Two key features should be incorporated into the guidelines:

- increases in assets accounts like stock and accounts receivable, consume cash, while decreases generate cash
- increases in liability and stock holders' equity accounts, such as accounts payable and bank loans, generate cash, while decreases consume cash (see Table 5.4).

Needs for Working Capital =
Stocks
+
Accounts receivable
-
Accounts payable

Working Capital =
Profits
+
Long-term debt + Capital
-
Fixed assets

CASH IS FACT, PROFIT IS OPINION

Pursuing increased sales growth without taking account of what effect it has on cash will result in misleading signals of marketing performance. As a profit centre, a marketing unit can significantly improve its cash situation by assessing the impact of its sales decisions on its cash flows. A more detailed set of guidelines could be drawn up to assist the marketing units to manage their cash position and not focus excessively on future profits that might never materialize if they spend their time 'doing things right' – ie marketing sales at any cost to the organization, rather than 'doing the right things' – ie identifying the limits of the working capital and managing the customer business from a cash perspective. Any routine decision by the sales staff can trigger a cash-dilutive situation; equally, cash growth can be generated by paying more attention to working-capital needs versus working-capital sources (see Tables 5.3 and 5.4).

Table 5.2 *Traditional asset accounts*

Transactions	Decisions	Effect on cash
Accounts receivable increase	Extend additional credit or allow longer time for customer to settle account; delay in getting invoices out to customer	-
Accounts receivable decrease	Faster collection of money owed by customer	+
Stock increase	Acquire or produce additional stock	-
Stock decrease	Sell some or all of stock	+
Pre-paid expenses increase	Pay more in advance for rent of warehouse, or travel	-
Pre-paid expenses decrease	Pay less in advance for rental, travel, sales promotion	+

Table 5.3 *Traditional current liability accounts*

Transactions	Decisions	Effect on cash
Accounts payable increase	Acquire more goods or services on credit or request later payment	+
Accounts payable decrease	Acquire less goods or services on credit or payment made sooner	-
Accrued payables increase	Stall payment of debts	+
Accrued payables decrease	Make more frequent payments to creditors	-

GROWTH = CASH USE; CONTRACTION = CASH FLOW

Over a protracted period of time the rate of self-financiable growth will be closely linked to the operating cash cycle of the business. The marketing unit, as a profit centre, needs to invest cash in stock, sell its goods, then deliver them and invoice the clients. It must subsequently wait to collect the accounts receivable before putting the cash to use again in the business. Clearly, the length of the operating cycle determines the rapidity with which the cash can be re-deployed: the shorter the cycle, all things being equal, the sooner the marketing unit has the cash available and the faster it can grow on the basis of internal sources. Failure to do so means that alternative sources of finance need to be found, diminishing the ultimate profit level, due to interest payments.

Consider the simplified profit and cashflow profile of the marketing operation in Table 5.4.

Table 5.4 *Profit and cashflow profile*

Income statement	Global amounts	Unit amounts	Operating cash cycle	
	(£)	(£)		
Revenue	1,000	1.00	Stock	80 days
Cost of sales	700	0.70	Accounts receivable	90 days
Overheads	250	0.25	Operating cash cycle	170 days
Profit	50	0.05	Working capital	140 days

The unit holds its stock on average for 80 days before selling it. Its customers pay the bill some 90 days later, resulting in a cash operating cycle of 170 days. Offsetting this is the supplier's trade credit period of 30 days, thereby creating a real investment in working capital of 140 days. In addition to stock and accounts receivable, the unit has also more regular overhead expenses of £250, such as selling costs, sales staff salaries, etc. occurring through the 170-day cycle. The amount of cash tied up in the operating cycle can now be calculated on the basis of the above statements. In order to generate £1 of sales, £0.70 is needed for operating expenses linked to stock (which corresponds to the cost of sales). But since this amount is tied up for only 140 days, the cash employed for cost of goods is:

£0.70 x 140/170 = £0.57

Equally, to generate £1 of sales, an overhead expense amount of £0.25 needs to be invested. The average overhead expense outstanding over the period (170/2 = 85) can be arrived at as follows:

£0.25 x 85/170 = £0.125

Thus the marketing unit needs to employ a combined investment in cost of goods sold and overhead expenses over the operating cycle of:

£0.57 + £0.1250 = £0.695

that is, for each £1 of sales generated in the cycle, the unit is required to invest nearly 70 pence.

DOES SO MUCH STOCK NEED TO BE CARRIED?

Reducing the cash burden imposed by holding stock can be minimized by managing the business differently.

- Ordering stock only on the basis of firm orders from the customer.
- Having the supplier fund the stock until the marketing unit has sold it.

- Focusing more carefully on slow-moving and high-value items in the product range – if 80 per cent of stock value is tied up in 20 per cent of items, better management of these items will be critical to reduce the resources (cash) 'immobilized' in such items.
- Offering two prices to clients: (1) on credit from stock based on one price, (2) cash sale with a slight delay (where the unit does not supply from stock), based on a 5 per cent discount.

The key issue the marketing unit must bear in mind is that carrying excessive stock and accounts receivable can be damaging to the business in cash terms, unless the unit has sufficient sources it can rely on.

KEY ISSUES

- Marketing performance must go beyond antiquated sales volume and revenue targets to take account of the costs of sustaining these activities. Many marketing activities are pursued at a cost level that is disproportionate to the ultimate value of the earnings.
- Effectiveness of marketing activities is measured in terms of 'doing the right things', rather than 'doing things right'. Variance analysis provides only part of the answer.
- The traditional revenue centre status of marketing department ignores the profit imperative: the need to take account of the cost of sales and marketing expenses and their combined potential in generating profitable sales.
- Increased marketing expenditures within the organization should be made in the expectation of enhanced sales revenue: trade-offs between expenses and revenues will be part of the decision-making process.
- Profit centres allow marketing units to (1) understand the cost structure of providing products and services, (2) seek the least-cost means of producing and servicing for their customer base, from either outside or internal sources, (3) be more selective in accepting certain types of business given the costs and complexity of servicing, (4) keep the fixed cost nature of business to a minimum level, and (5) contribute to company profits.

■ Increased sales and marketing activities absorb cash in the business; unless sales and buying transactions can be matched, excess cash outflows in the long term will drain the business of resources.

■ Decisions taken at local sales level can be sources of cash-drainage – increased investments in accounts receivable, extension of credit, the build-up of stocks, etc; profits are not always indicative of how much cash is available in the business.

■ Self-financiable growth has to be calculated in relation to the company's working capital base and the means of financing this growth: growth constitutes cash use, whereas contraction generates cash.

■ Excessive stocks, accounts receivable and work-in-progress represents 'immobilized' cash in the business – unless stocks are released and customers pay promptly, no cash will be generated.

■ Increases in asset accounts such as stock and accounts receivable, consume cash; increases in liability and stock holders' equity accounts, such as accounts payable and loans, generate cash.

BIBLIOGRAPHY

Blackstone Franks & Co, Chartered Accountants (UK), 'Cash, cash, cash: 39 of the best ideas'

A Cane, 'Ericsson claims lead as pre-tax jumps', *Financial Times* (30 October 1996)

N Churchill and J Mullins, 'Ensuring the operating cash cycle is moved into the correct gear', *Financial Times* Mastering Enterprise, 8

F Evans, 'A road map to your financial report', *AMA Management Review* (October 1993)

Horngren, Foster and Datar, *Cost Accounting: A managerial emphasis*, Prentice-Hall (9th edn) (1997)

L Kellaway, 'Keeping hold of the customer', *Financial Times* (25 March 1993)

F Lefley, 'Capital investments: the financial appraisal profile', *Certified Accountant* (June 1997)

J O'Hare, 'Controlling working capital', *Accountancy* (International edn) (October 1997)

P Martin, 'It's the revenues, stupid', *Financial Times* (27 December 1996)

R Peston, 'Rules to reveal where profit may mean loss', *Financial Times* (27 September 1991).

M Ullman, 'Routes to a successful turnround', *Financial Times* Mastering Enterprises, 5

6

MAKING BETTER USE OF INFORMATION TECHNOLOGY IN MARKETING

The marketing function is immersed in an Information Age with remote access to information about practically every aspect of its globalized marketplace. With a simple click of the mouse, marketing executives can scan Web pages on the Internet to find out what the competition is offering and saying to customers. They can tap into multiple corporate databases to learn more about the customers' buying habits. Corporate e–mail connections provide them with links to almost everyone in the value–chain from the suppliers right through to the customers' home.

The challenge, as management guru Peter Drucker once commented, is knowing how to distinguish between data and knowledge, and between IT and information. As increasing quantities of data about the market and consumers become available, and the free flow of information over the Net between buyers and sellers increases, marketing heads must be alert to the opportunities and threats the Internet phenomena presents; it is clear that they can no longer remain indifferent.

INTERACTIVE MARKETING

One of the most important information technology (IT) developments in recent years is the emergence of interactive marketing. As a form of continuing dialogue with the consumer that is not subject to the traditional promotion lag, its potential lies in considerably cutting the cost of doing business; more importantly, it allows closer links between the supplier and customer, thus eliminating the middlemen such as distributors. The flagship of interactive marketing is the Internet, which is already being touted as the engine of growth for the IT market. IT marketing experts now view the Internet as another sales channel to market and promote products and services, especially over the Web. The 'cybermarketing' phenomenon now includes video games, TV home shopping, mail and telephone marketing, through CD–ROMs, on–line computer services and interactive kiosks right up to the ultimate dream of many marketers, shopping by computer.

The growth of interactive marketing and media has been explosive. Statistics from the USA show that about 40 million households have a PC and roughly half of those possess a modem to connect to the telecommunications network. Some 10 million people are connected to the Internet, either at home or work, and 9 million households are now connected to some form of on–line service. The figures are lower in Europe, but the trends are broadly similar (see Table 6.1). The fastest–growing application is the World Wide Web (WWW) that has provided rapid access to multimedia material – text, voice, and graphics – around the globe.

Table 6.1 *Users of on–line services per 1,000 inhabitants*

Country	Usage 1997	Predictions for 2000
Spain	21	64
Italy	24	70
Japan	41	93
Germany	76	156
UK	84	158
France	99	169
USA	183	303

Sources: W3B/Commerzbank, Globus.

Internet usage is predicted to grow dramatically within the next decade, with the number of PC users wired to the Net at around 1 billion. For the present, confirmed subscribers world–wide number between 60 and 80 million, according to a Sofres survey, with wide variations: France, for example, has some 500,000 subscribers. The available of such 'captive audiences' suggests a formidable marketing opportunity for buying and selling over the Internet. Forecasts prepared by IDC Research indicate that the volume of on–line commerce will reach $150 billion by 2000, climbing to more than $1 trillion by the year 2010, if, as some observers say, the Internet can be made more attractive to entice people who are not computer–literate.

THE INTERNET CONNECTION

Corporate Web aficionados assert that marketing is well placed to benefit from cybermarketing, but that companies must get organized now to meet this challenge. Interactive marketing is seen as having a significant impact in reinforcing three key fundamental roles in marketing:

- informing customer groups about the company, its products and its policies
- cultivating brand–awareness, differentiating the brands from competitors and establishing preference among customers
- reinforcing customer confidence in order to generate orders and sales.

US corporations have led the charge in adopting cybermarketing practices. An AMACOM (American Management Association) study of 1995 points to some tangible benefits in the way marketing can reduce costs and boost revenues as a result of the Internet.

Making more effective use of the marketing budget

Printing, storing and distribution costs associated with sales catalogues, brochures and trade directories can be reduced. Updates can be implemented with greater facility. When used as a conduit for millions of electronic messages to selective groups of customers, the cost of Internet e–mail is independent of how far the message must travel; this makes it a big cost saver for international communications compared with telephone calls, facsimiles or conventional mail.

Time is saved

Information about products, after–sales enquiries, quotes, availability of stocks, etc is accessible immediately to key marketing staff in the office or in the field. Waiting around time to print and mail details is eliminated and the customer has an answer quickly. From the customer perspective, using the Net as a virtual shop has its attractions: electronic stores are open 24 hours a day, seven days a week, making it particularly suitable for the so–called 'too busy, two–income families'.

An additional buying point is established

The customer can now order products via cyberspace, thereby avoiding commuting to the point–of–sale, parking hassles, the risk that the product is out of stock when they get to the store, etc. Expanding the choices available, both product and processes will add to customer satisfaction.

Information is more readily accessible

Faced with wider choices of products and prices, consumers want more information before they make a decision; an Internet Web site provides this vital link in the decision–making chain of events prior to the buying act.

Broadening international reach

Companies, particularly small ones, can compete on a least–cost basis across frontiers and thus expand their international clientele. Cross–cultural differences no longer feature high on the list of impediments to expansion.

As a marketing tool, the Internet is a formidable means of gathering information about consumers, their tastes and their buying behaviour. Not surprisingly, the IT industry has led the way in offering demonstration versions of new products to Internet users over the WWW connection. This offers something more vital than a cursory presentation of available products: feedback on the product and its teething problems is used by researchers to fine–tune the product's features, and a ready–made list of potential customers for the company's product also emerges. In addition, IT companies provide on–line 'help desks' to assist customers in solving their problems. This can alert manufacturers to the potential problems that can be expected in the national launch stage, as well as feedback on the positive and negative features of the product.

The existence of this tool also presents a challenge to suppliers. The Internet can be used by retailers to gather information about their customers. Armed with improved customer information, an on–line retailer could conceivably exert more pressure on suppliers by demanding larger discounts, thereby diluting manufacturers' margins. Another option open to on–line retailers is the forging of closer links with suppliers, by co–operating and sharing information aimed at reducing processing errors, lead–times and stocks tying up working capital.

The most visible impact in marketing has been the Internet's ability to create an alternative sales distribution channel thereby reducing costs. In 1997, Apple announced the opening of its first 'Internet store', a Web site through which customers can order 'built–to–order' Macintosh computers, software and related products. This emulates an earlier Internet store concept launched by Dell Computer, one of Apple's most successful competitors, who offer essentially the same functions. Dell has generated nearly $1billion in sales via the Internet, about 10 per cent of its total sales in 1997. Marketing analysts warn, however, that such moves may risk antagonizing the traditional retail dealers of PCs and software.

A FORGOTTEN MARKET RESEARCH TOOL

In the enthusiasm that has accompanied Internet marketing, consumer product manufacturers have overlooked another use of the Internet: its potential as a market research tool. Statistics compiled by Nielsen and ASI Research reveal that in the USA some 28 per cent of consumer–packaged products are sold to households which have Internet access. In some product categories, Internet users represent over 40 per cent of purchases. The Internet audience segment is thus an attractive, albeit untested, target market for many consumer products, and can be used for testing responses for all varieties of new products. Suppliers can exploit this information about their customers to tailor their current products and services, and eventually create a sense of community amongst their customers. This latter approach was used by Amazon, the first on–line book seller with 1997 sales over the Web of over $148 million. The 2 million people who visited Amazon's Website in December 1997 also had the possibility to submit book reviews.

Vast savings in travel and staff time can be accrued by developing on–line focus groups to test new products with immediate responses spread across geographical boundaries. On–line surveys and opinion polls can be used where demographic information is needed to correct skewed response rates. Multiple–question menus can obtain vital information, each one triggering off another fresh line of questions. The on–line or telephone 'help desks' can also provide sources of information gleaned from the consumer of the product, which is then fed back to the manufacturer.

The main attraction of the Net as a market research tool is the ability to collect information about potential, and existing consumers, who not only 'visit' the Web site, but who go further and 'click through' data by simply clicking on an advertisement on a Web page to get more information.

The main impediment of the Internet use for market research purposes – and, indeed, as a promotional vehicle – is the narrow demographic user profile. The Web is heavily skewed towards users who are male, between the ages of 25 and 35 and earning above–average incomes. For companies selling to these demographic segments, the Internet is a formidable means for gathering information and promoting products. It is less obvious as a promotional tool for the older consumer or those who do not have access to, or have any enthusiasm for, the Internet.

To be sure, drawing new users into the information age is still a preoccupation for the European and US high–tech industry. Over 60 per cent of US households do not own a PC, and this figure is higher in other parts of the world (see Table 6.2).

Table 6.2 *Number of households with electronic equipment, 1994 (per cent)*

	France	Germany	Italy	UK
VCR	64.0	65.0	46.0	88.0
PC	14.4	29.5	15.7	18.6
Fax	3.0	4.0	2.0	2.0

Sources: Observatoire du multimedia (Sofres) and I&T magazine (EU).

The task will not be easy; while the USA still holds a sizeable lead in the ownership of PCs, about 70 per cent of PCs purchased by US consumers, for instance, are bought by people who already have at least one PC at home. They are replacing, upgrading or adding to their home computing systems. The former head of Apple Computer, Gil Ammelio, noted in a 1996 Financial Times interview that 'only about 7 per cent of the world's population uses a computer, or has access to one... within five years, this may rise to 15 or 16 per cent. But what about the other 85 per cent?'

According to a world–wide survey conducted by the Brussels–based International Research Institutes (IIRS), the ownership of modems – the communications devises that enable PCs to be connected to the Internet on–line services – is highest in the USA (58 per cent) and lowest in southern Europe, dipping to 19 per cent in Italy. Overall the number of adults owning a modem and therefore having access to the Internet is still very low, averaging about 15 per cent in most countries except the USA. A study written by Fletcher Research and sponsored by McKinsey indicated that the 9 per cent of Britons who use the Internet do so chiefly at work, unlike the US users.

The same IRIS study conducted over 18 countries reiterates the general trend: Internet users are predominately males under the age of 55 in the upper-income category. Internet awareness remains its highest in North America and Northern European countries (see Table 6.3). Home connections to the Internet are claimed by 19 per cent of US respondents, followed by Canada (18 per cent). Elsewhere, Australia leads with 12 per cent home connections, followed by Finland (10 per cent), and Sweden and the Netherlands sharing 9 per cent each. The overwhelming place of access still remains the workplace. More disturbingly, the study shows significantly less usage of the Internet by women. Cybermarketing experts point to the ominous fact that while 80 per cent of shopping is still carried out by women, 80 per cent of Internet users are men.

CYBERSPACE MARKETING

Getting started

Low Web penetration in many parts of the world, together with much–publicized cybermarketing difficulties in transforming it into a profitable activity, has led to the perception that the Internet is a volatile sales channel. However, the free flow of information via cyberspace across national frontiers now signals that corporations cannot continue to ignore the impact of the Web – least of all the marketing function.

The key factor in successful marketing in cyberspace is the focus on providing information and not using it to sell products. Some experts see Web sites as being no different from having the company's telephone number listed: the reality is that the company still has to do some basic marketing. Potential consumers still have to be told that the Web site number exists, and people have to be given a reason to visit the site. Experienced cybermarketers point to a number of practical guidelines in getting value out of marketing on the Internet.

Consider identifying e-mail subscription lists associated with the company's offerings or topic of interest

By subscribing to these lists, the company participates in the cyberspace segment where the potential customers are gathered, and informs them that a Web site exists. A compelling reason to go to that site has to be developed; this can be done by providing free information.

Develop a long-term relationship with potential customers by offering free information

A survey in the USA found that 71 per cent of people went on-line to get information. If there is a sustainable level of information provided by the company, the 'visitors' will keep returning to the site. A relationship based on familiarization and relevant information can lead to a business relationship developing over time. On-line information sites with copious details about products that potential clients may wish to buy could be the first step towards transforming them into an on-line shopper. Sometimes the Web facility can support the main marketing thrust. Business Week, owned by US information group McGraw-Hill, claims it gets about 300,000 'hits' a month for its electronic version. As a result the paper version has been enhanced and a new stream of revenue has been created.

Avoid relying exclusively on graphical presentations, as text is also important in cyberspace

Not every browser has the equipment to see graphics on–line because of the different types of Web browsers employed. What is loaded on to the Web site may not look the same to each person who visits the site. Graphics, taking up more data than words, can lead to excessively long advertisements on the Web, and be frustrating for consumers who have to wait some time for it to be downloaded; this can drive them to another company's site. Research shows that many Net users will abandon a page that takes more than 30 seconds to display, or switch off the image–loading feature in their Web browser, diminishing the real information or sales attractiveness of the page.

Minimize cluttering the site with information made up of a hybrid of product and corporate information

A potential consumer seeking a list of dealers in his geographical region does not want to spend an inordinate amount of time wading through irrelevant information before finding what he wants; inflicting the annual report and accounts on unsuspecting consumers may be unwelcome.

Use the site to test the effectiveness of the marketing message

The Internet offers the marketer the possibility to develop campaigns incrementally over time, unlike a direct–mail campaign, which is redundant once the mail–shot letter and envelopes have been ordered from the printer. The Net advertiser could begin with two variations of the same offer, monitor the response each day and amend the message at no extra cost until it comes up with a more successful version.

Exploit the site to tailor the company's advertising in specifically specialized ways

A Web visitor surfing sites for information on specific themes like whiskey could be offered a banner ad for J&B upon searching for sites on the beverage. Again, the effect is one of providing information or a reminder that the customer needs to stock up in whiskey (and associating it with a J&B purchase).

Build a more accurate profile via the Website of the company's targeted potential consumers

Everything that occurs during a Net session is recorded in an electronic file somewhere for future use. Not only do companies know how many people visited the site to read the message, but also how many were interested enough to click the ad. Specifically targeted messages can be developed to reach a pool of potential users, with less wastage in marketing resource terms.

Generating visits to the Web site

Being a passive marketing medium, the Internet site will play a more important role in providing information rather than as a sales vehicle. The challenge is in finding ways to lure consumers to the site, and keep people coming back for a weekly instalment of information.

For companies embarking on cybermarketing activities for the first time, generating visits to the Website is imperative. Visits can be encouraged by registering the URL (Uniform Resource Locator, or address) with the Internet and the global Web search engines. These search engines function as catalogues for Web sites, enabling users to find the sites they are looking for with greater ease and rapidity. Beyond that, it requires good marketing skills to 'sell' the medium. Promoting the Internet Web site should also be part of an overall communications policy of the company: the URL Web site address and the e–mail address should be incorporated into as many of the company's identity objects as possible:

- letterheads
- business cards
- flyers and brochures
- fax cover sheets
- press communiqués
- company publications – annual report, user manuals, etc.
- mail–shots and advertising.

Generic mailboxes can also be arranged for different parts of the organization the customer may wish to contact depending on his or her needs – ie info@ accounts@, and sales@, etc. More importantly, the Internet medium should not be looked upon as a stand–alone marketing tool; it has to be fully integrated with the company's brand marketing thrust and image.

Commercial e-mail

A useful marketing derivative of the Internet system to cultivate dialogue with the customer is the availability of commercial e-mail – sometimes referred to as d-mail, after 'direct mail'. US marketers, in particular, are excited about the prospects of using d-mail to identify new customers, and in a selective way, to keep in discrete touch with them. A flower services group in the USA use the Internet postal service to remind customers of important dates such as birthdays. With over 200,000 reminders sent via d-mail to clients in one year, florists using the medium have found that Net customers buy, on average, three times more than other customer groups and spend about $11 more on each transaction.

CYBERMARKETING

The hidden costs

Constant need to change and update
As Internet usage accelerates on a global scale, cybermarketing experts are quick to point out that the control of access to the medium is increasingly concentrated in the hands of a limited number of owners. This has made it more expensive to create a website that is a household name, capable of attracting people who are used to visiting the site. Significant marketing investments are required by companies to launch a value–added website, unless a partner can be found with a well–known brand and website or online service that is a regular 'destination' for users; this could provide the opportunity at less cost to 'piggyback' on an existing website to build business.

The Internet is not considered by many marketers as being a direct point–of–sale medium but more suitable for 'advertising' information. Whatever use is made of the company Web site, the activity represents added workloads for the marketing department and pressure to constantly change and update the content. All this entails heavy staff–related costs. In addition, the momentum has to be sustained. One beer company ran a competition on its Web site which upon reaching its closing date, failed to be replaced or updated. The reaction by its users was one of annoyance and unfavourable publicity for the Web site.

'Netiquette'
The use of the Internet as a marketing tool requires a good understanding of its technology. A KPMG survey from 1996 showed that 60 per cent of UK marketing directors described their knowledge of Internet technology as poor or very poor. This can translate into a series of marketing *faux pas*. Within the marketing unit, care needs to be taken in adhering to *de facto* acceptable Internet commercial behaviour, so as to avoid antagonizing a customer with, for instance, blanket–bombing e–mail, clogging up the network. Net users show a distinct distaste for junk mail; since consumers pay for the time they spend on–line, they may not want to waste their time on unsolicited mail.

Start–up and maintenance costs
A budget has to be allocated for start–up costs and the 'maintenance' of the Web site with frequent information updates. Some companies have discovered that setting up a Web site is more complicated than originally envisaged. Building up databases, developing a user–friendly format and creating links between various pages require computer–programming skills – all of which can be costly. The cost of running a company site varies greatly, depending on the type of hardware and telecommunications used. Basic connection services in the USA range can be as much as $20 a month. Connections with higher speeds of interaction can raise this figure to $1,000 a month. With constant updating and e–mail activities linked to the company's Internet site, an additional full–time staff person to manage the medium should also be added to the costs. The maintenance and upkeep costs need to be accurately budgeted and can cover four broad areas:

- site maintenance and development
- monitoring and feedback
- updating
- visibility and site traffic analysis.

Global reach
The Internet's global reach – information is accessible from anywhere in the world – can pose certain problems in geographically dispersed organizations selling similar products in clearly defined territories. A case in point is the French company featuring information on its Web pages about new or existing products sold only

in France. This could lead to diminishing sales in other EU countries where customers realize that currently available products in their own country may have become obsolete, or are simply more expensive. Customer relations will suffer as a result, not to mention the company's image.

Mass–market penetration

For the mass market, Internet penetration is nowhere near the saturation coverage provided by TV, the press, magazines, direct mail and posters. Figures showing the number of Internet hosts per thousand inhabitants in the major developed economies (see Table 6.3), underline the fact that most parts of Europe have a long way to go before they reach US levels. In addition, the Net advertising costs, for mass–market brands, are not cheap. Though the rates are increasingly flexible, cost/1,000 Net viewers reached are significantly higher than those offered by traditional media. The fundamental question the marketing people have to ask is: How technically literate are our customers? Simply put, if a company's customers are not that way inclined, having a Web site may do little to improve profitability, and may represent a waste of resources.

A new opportunity?

With some 23 million households now connected to the Internet, translating into multiple family users, the appeal of electronic commerce has grown into another point–of–sale option. In the USA, e–commerce seems to have attained critical mass. Whereas less than 40 million people were connected to the Web in 1996, there are now over 100 million. Big retailers like Wal–Mart offer products over the World Wide Web and have launched virtual reality shopping facilities. Supermarket groups have also come on line and allowed consumers to do some grocery shopping at home. But companies are finding that the Internet is not suitable for selling everything; some offerings sell better than others. Consumption patterns show that on–line purchases fall into three categories.

■ Computer software and hardware, which were the first goods to be widely available on–line and remain the most commonly purchased over the Net.

- Travel–related items, such as airline tickets are popular, with many airlines allowing customers to examine schedules and buy tickets on–line; US independent travel agencies have seen their share of airline reservations drop from 80 per cent to 52 per cent as airlines adopt the Web to sell directly to clients.
- Leisure goods, with books, music CDs and video cassettes representing the hot items; record retailers believe that the on–line market for CDs is potentially extremely profitable because Web site overheads are lower than those of a conventional store.

In spite of the publicity surrounding electronic commerce in recent years, it remains surprisingly small. In the USA, electronic selling is estimated to be worth about $5.8 billion in 1997 – a tiny fraction billion(0.01 per cent) of the $2500 billion retail market. In Europe, figures are closer to 0.02 per cent of retail sales. A Consumer Direct Cooperative investigation into US on–line shopping habits in 1997 showed that the figure for households regularly using on–line services for groceries and related goods is currently 200,000; this is expected to rise to between 15 million and 20 million by 2007. The bulk of on–line buyers demographically match the profile of Internet users in general; so, supposedly, technologically literate young men buy most on–line. By 2000, according to Forrester Research, a technology consulting and research group, it is anticipated that a third of Internet shoppers will be women.

Another current impediment is the security risk in paying on–line, resulting from computer hackers breaking into the systems. Cyberspace marketers say that electronic shopping represents about the same risk as giving a credit card number to a catalogue merchant. In any event, almost all reputable retailers use some sort of encryption technology to protect credit card information.

As interactive shopping becomes more user–friendly and easy to access, impediments such as consumers' desire to actually handle the products may diminish. But the current limiting factor for retailing groups is the high cost of running an on–line store – ie delivering goods to consumers' homes. Some have persuaded on–line customers to order and pay for their weekly groceries by computer. The order is then assembled by their local store where the customer picks it up by car at a store collection point on the way to pick up the children at school or on the way home from work. Cyberspace marketing experts assert that some 20 per cent of the product price in retailing is tied up in store costs and overheads. Electronic shopping groups can reduce these charges by stripping out the property cost of the high street or suburbia stores, and dispense with upkeep staff, security and stock management functions, and deliver directly from warehouses to customers. The 20 per cent saving could then be used for technology and distribution, following a similar *modus operandi* employed by the mail–order companies. The major challenge facing e–commerce is in providing a social dimension to on–line shopping at a time when marketing people still believe that 'folks enjoy the experience of shopping'.

THE INTERNATIONAL IMPLICATIONS OF CYBERMARKETING

For companies considering offering their wares on–line across borders, two relevant marketing issues require careful attention.

- Brands and dealerships may be the property of one company in the USA and another in the EU. All current supplier–distribution agreements should be examined to ensure that there are no restrictions concerning relevant geographical or marketing channels. Failure to address the question of competition in markets which franchise and distribution agreements restrict one party from entering can result in litigation.
- Warranties provided with the product or the software used to create the Internet store and to enable the customers to access the site should be reviewed. Errors in transactions over the Net brought much of the system to a temporary halt in the USA in 1997: the cost of the market being temporarily inaccessible, lost orders or customers being misinformed can be high.

THE FUTURE OF CYBERMARKETING

The marketing industry, while not in the category of virtual reality shopping *stricto sensu*, is being profoundly influenced by it. The reason is that the Internet, unlike other promotional tools before it, is an interactive medium, capable of being 'customized' to each viewer. The Internet is conceptually easier to use in targeting potentially interested consumers and communicating with them. The key word is 'communicating', and, as such, it is increasingly being seen as a support mechanism to back up the core marketing programme. As an advertising medium, the take–up has been slow. Total Internet advertising revenues have been disappointing: $267 million in 1996, compared to $33 billion spent on TV advertising in the USA alone. An increasing number of publishers and information providers are planning to start charging for access to some of the information they make available on the Internet. While having a Web site is almost essential for publishers, economics is also a factor to be considered as publishers continue to lose money on Web site marketing, despite on–line advertising. The continuing difficulty in measuring the effectiveness of Net ads against the investments in hardware, software and upkeep costs has resulted in a wait–and–see mode by media experts, pending developments in cyberspace.

KNOW THY CUSTOMER, AND HOW IT CAN HELP

Corporate databases

The most useful IT development to affect marketing, in recent times, has been the realization that corporate databases contain a goldmine of valuable information about the customer; techniques such as data warehouses and data mining now enable companies to establish a detailed picture of their customers' profile and needs and, hopefully, provide them with a better service. Such developments, in the eyes of many experienced marketers, have taken the marketing function back to the earlier, more rewarding, days when customers shopped in small stores where their tastes and preferences were known, and shop owners were able to cater for their needs.

Table 6.3 *Internet hosts per 1,000 inhabitants, July 1996*

(1995 population data used to calculate 1996 hosts per 1,000 inhabitants)

Australia	21.98	Austria	8.83
Belgium	4.28	Canada	14.33
Denmark	14.73	Finland	54.27
France	3.27	Germany	6.70
Greece	1.21	Ireland	5.99
Italy	2.00	Japan	3.96
Mexico	0.22	Netherlands	13.89
New Zealand	22.06	Norway	27.75
Portugal	1.77	Spain	1.59
Sweden	21.10	Switzerland	14.59
UK	9.90	USA	31.26

Source: Network Wizards at HYPERLINK http://www.nw.com/

With the advent of large multiple chains of super–retailers in the 1960s and 1970s, store owners have relinquished their individual-ized attention *vis–à–vis* customers in favour of mass–marketing techniques. Markets that were once a mass society, with similar tastes across the board, have now evolved to being multicultural societies; this has rendered retail activities more localized. Most marketing risks becoming highly unselective – and thus resource–wasteful. Discerning customers of French cuisine are not thought to be likely to eat at a fast–food outlet but are subject, nevertheless, to TV ads for hamburgers and soft drinks. A high proportion of the fast–food company's advertising budget will, however, be spent on people who will conceivably never enter a fast–food outlet. The same argument can be applied to a wide range of other consumer products and services.

Cheaper and more sophisticated database technologies are now making it possible to build huge central repositories of infor-mation about every aspect of the customer. Improved target mar-keting allows companies to reward loyal customers and avoid wasting resources on promotions and products to unlikely buyers. From a cost and competitive perspective, such information, and its effective use, will be critical at a time when the popular mar-keting adage about keeping and retaining customers is factored in: it costs five times as much to replace a customer as it does to keep one.

Data warehousing

A data warehouse collects an assortment of data stored in the disparate corporate electronic systems – billing invoices in the accounting unit, customer records in customer services, and sales figures from the sales department – and collates it all into one database. The warehouse architecture consists of a separate relational database of integrated detailed historical data. This information can then be explored to gain insights into the customer and develop new micro–marketing options. Determining customer behaviour from past patterns, hidden in the data accumulated by different parts of the organization, enables the company to determine detailed marketing initiatives and target their customers more accurately. Exploiting such information has led to some interesting results.

- Large supermarket groups analyse cash register data to learn about what customers typically buy at the same time. Improved floor and shelf layouts can thus be devised to facilitate buying decisions associated with end of week purchases of the typical working woman, such as sliced bread and coffee.
- Companies can better discriminate between valued customers whom they wish to retain and those who are likely to be less valuable over time. Such tracking techniques enabled one US retailer to identify a specific valued–customer category it calls 'fashion guard', comprising middle–aged shoppers who spend $5,000 annually at their store. By contrast, it also revealed a 'value–customer' category of less apparent interest, who shopped only at sales, and the more elderly couple type of customer, who purchased items selectively. Each store could then be described by the dominance of certain categories of customers and the marketing approach adjusted accordingly. Similar techniques are employed by some airlines that use their databases to upgrade frequent clients to business class compared to occasional flyers.
- Companies can enhance the response rate to their direct–mail campaigns by being more selective of households to whom mail is sent. The financial services industry has pioneered extensively in this area, as the largest users of direct mail, enabling them to put more effort into marketing to good prospects and less to addressing the mass market. The use of existing customer bases has turned banks and insurance com-

panies away from the expensive and frequently unrewarding task of trying to win over new customers whom they know little about. Information systems have been restructured to turn policy records into customer databases to determine what sort of people buy what sort of financial product. Some software can spot patterns in people's life–styles and identify life events that trigger key financial decisions, like house purchases with the arrival of a second child. This has resulted in:

– better targeting of the customer
– fewer mail shots sent out
– a higher response rate
– a higher conversion rate to new business.

The methods of collecting information on customers can vary from one industry to another. Catalogue–sales companies can build sales histories that go back years via a mail–order database. More frequently, retailers entice customers to fill in a card about themselves, ostensibly to inform them about impending sales. In reality, a database can be built up of addresses and matched with demographic analysis of age and life–styles based on home location. However, retail tracking reveals more about the customer when done with magnetic stripe cards, such as store discount cards, that automatically register purchases in the computer system. Information gathered in this way can benefit the retailer in a number of ways:

■ the impact of a special promotion in–store can be assessed
■ defected customers can be identified and encouraged to return
■ non–users of complementary or associated items offered by the retailer can be identified
■ the selection of products and services can be modified to suit the customer profile
■ the seasonality of the business can be examined to get the product mix right and build more appropriate marketing response
■ spending habits of different demographic and cultural categories of customers can be monitored, enabling more targeted offers and customer service.

Analysing the data

The ensuing task of analysing the data is vital. The marketer can divide the data into segments using 'data–mining' techniques that can sift, collate and burrow into the database. In a retail environment, for instance, this would consist of segmenting its customers into multiple but manageable, different groups or market categories on issues like their propensity to spend more money, whether they frequent the store to purchase their principal or top–up groceries each week, or how sensitive they are to price and promotions. Different marketing strategies can then be devised to respond to their different needs.

The information collected should result in more focused direct marketing policies, as consumers will receive only information that is genuinely of interest to them. For example, a customer segment identified as having an interest in golf might be interested in receiving a catalogue of golf clothing items. Customers can, obviously, choose not to be sent any direct–mail shots, but research shows that consumers are more irritated with direct marketing resulting from unsolicited mail that is of absolutely no interest to them.

A customer database can also support efforts aimed at retaining existing customers. An airline might, for example, learn from its database of customers that a valued–traveller is a keen gardener; on his next trip on the airline, the company would ensure that a copy of the latest edition of *House and Gardens* was waiting on board for him to read. The travel and tourism industry have begun to use their IT systems for tasks that go beyond reservations and billing, to track their customers' spending over time in different hotels. Hotels are now less concerned with the value of their properties than the value over time of regular customers: frequent visitors are worth more preferential treatment and are cultivated with rooms set up the way they like them, offered discounts or suggestions of vacation breaks away from home. With the help of improved information about their customers, hotel chains have created different sub–brands to cater to customers' different preferences at different times. More regular guests staying away from HQ for weeks on business, for instance, can now be targeted with extended–stay hotel packages.

But the human touch may still be necessary...

Critics of data–warehousing techniques point to ethics of companies holding information about the customers' life–styles and habits. Others underline the idiosyncratic nature of customers' decisions to enter a store with the intention of buying, motivations which are not elucidated with information from the database. And even when they do enter the store, experienced sales staff point to customers being notoriously capricious; frequently, they do not know what they want. Databases will not persuade the customer nor help to replace the selling job so essential in guiding the customer to the ultimate buying act.

Marketing specialists, while impressed with the analytical abilities of databases, are concerned that they should not be used at the expense of intuition and judgement. As technology costs fall further, there is a risk of being seduced and overwhelmed by the power of database marketing. The KPMG survey of 1997 found high levels of dissatisfaction with existing IT systems in serving marketing needs, but low levels of awareness about the role of data warehousing.

Data warehouses can also be expensive and their sheer size makes them difficult to engineer. The most onerous part is extracting information from existing systems such as mainframes, which require special handling to get the data out and into a form that is accessible from the new warehouse: this can represent between 60 and70 per cent of the data warehouse cost. A stage further will require cleaning up the data, to deal with the diverse listing of the same customer in the company's various computer systems. Some reconciliation of data may have to be done as well to render it uniform: while the marketing department may segregate its territories into ten regions, the finance department may only have four areas.

SOME GUIDELINES

Definition of needs

A clear definition of needs is required both in terms of what the company wants to accomplish and what data is useful. This step must be marketing–driven rather than IT–driven. Those using the system may come from several levels within the organization – ie marketing, sales, stock control, etc – and must be involved at the input stage. Care has to be taken to ensure that each manager does not overload the system with personal additions that are nice to know but ineffectual in learning more about the customer: an information–cluttered warehouse quickly becomes useless.

Collecting of information

The collecting of information for the database from customer loyalty programmes or the use of electronic point–of–sale (EPOS) terminals should not disrupt or interfere with the day–to–day running of core activities within the store, especially at the checkout desk.

Direct mail

Direct mail, while benefiting from improved targeting arising from warehousing, has to be reviewed in the overall context of the corporate marketing plan. Does the organization possess expertise in direct marketing? What reaction can be expected from the customers to increasing levels of solicited and unsolicited mail? Could d–mail (electronic mail shots) be envisaged to reduce the costs of printing and postage?

Payback

The company should have a clear idea of the payback from such an investment and the realistic objectives these systems are to achieve. Only 16 per cent of respondents with data warehouses in the 1997 KPMG survey had measured their return on investment.

OTHER IT USES IN MARKETING

Call centres

In the telephony area, the use of call centres located in a central location, equipped with multilingual staff and telemarketing software, are expected to increase world–wide as the marketing activities, and associated costs, transcend international boundaries.

These systems handle outgoing direct selling activities, customers' responses to direct mail and after–sales service enquiries. The call centres improve the targeting of their direct selling by using information obtained from data warehouses and the results of data mining.

Intranet access

Some companies are creating extended channels by allowing their valued–customers access across the Internet to their internal Intranet and into their main business systems. Customers can check the product availability and delivery schedules, and enter orders directly, thus eliminating the cost of order–taking.

Sales and marketing software

The sales and marketing department can be supported and information sharing enhanced with the help of sales and marketing software. Such systems enable sales teams to manage campaigns, provide contact details, track and record customer interactions, monitor prospect status and help the sales team manage their time and co–ordinate their diverse actions more effectively. Corporate Intranets can also be pressed into service to allow sales staff to access all their support systems across the Internet – ie orders, delivery schedules, accounts receivables, etc (see Table 6.4).

Table 6.4 *IT systems supporting sales and marketing: future growth areas in order of priority*

■ Word processing and spreadsheets	■ e–mail
■ Portable computers	■ Internet/WWW
■ Contact management	■ Marketing databases
■ Mobile datacomms	■ Corporate Intranets
■ Market research package	■ Call centre/tele–marketing systems
■ Computer telephony	■ Geographic info system
■ Enterprise–wide systems	■ Sales force automation
■ Territory management software	

Source: Softworld survey: http//www.softinfo.com

MANAGING THE IT INVESTMENT FOR BETTER RESULTS

The marketing department, in common with other corporate units, has experienced the transformation of IT that has put real computing power on the desktop and into the hands of the end–user. Everyone from the senior marketing planning team to the sales staff in the field can now be linked up to inter–networked individual PCs.

This shift, however, has brought to the surface some disturbing facts about the cost of ownership of PCs themselves, at a time when senior management has become more concerned about obtaining optimum value from the IT investments and has devolved the responsibility for major expenditures on items like IT to local revenue centres. The 1995 US–based Gartner Research Group revealed that on average, the five–year cost of networked PC ownership has climbed from $19,000 in the mid–1980s to a figure in excess of $40,000. More revealing was the proportion of this cost attributable to the initial purchase: 20 per cent. The residual 80 per cent was absorbed by the on–going costs of ownership such as training, inventory tracking of hardware and software, software audits and updates, technical support and help desks, user downtime, data loss from system failure, etc.

Careful configuration of PCs within a diverse function like marketing is required in order to ensure an integrated system, capable of networking and sharing of information across departmental, and even geographic, boundaries. But this should not be guided by spontaneous decisions to upgrade the equipment in response to a fad. IT needs now have to be examined by marketing people with greater caution to avoid costly mistakes and wastage. A simple decision to upgrade the hardware to conform with Windows 95 (ie having PCs that are big enough and fast enough to run the software), for instance, can represent a costly exercise for a cost–conscious marketing department. The Gartner Research Group study puts the cost of upgrading to Windows 95 at between $400 and $3,000 per system, depending on the hardware configuration, training and software applications needed.

Failure to achieve the productivity gains originally envisaged as a result of IT investments has largely been blamed on buying the wrong sort of IT equipment, but experts are now saying that this is only part of the problem. Useless projects certainly waste resources, but more wasteful still is the inaccurate costing of IT vs human capital. Simplistic calculations of the trade–off between a staff member's salary saved *vis–à–vis* the cost of a computer do not take account of the longer–term costs associated with IT installations such as maintenance and programming; all of this can easily add up to the cost of the displaced staff.

For the profit–centre–focused marketing department with its own IT budget, six broad guidelines could be considered.

- Devise departmental–wide standards with the users, with recommended configurations, and ensure that they are compatible with the rest of the organization.
- Quantify the overall costs of IT in the department, including operations, technical support, maintenance and administration.
- Ensure that the right advice is sought on the appropriate IT equipment needed for the marketing operations and avoid being seduced by the latest fade in technology.
- Keep a track of the IT stock, both old and new software/equipment.
- Devise a plan for de–installing (disposal/removal) and remarketing (selling the old technology) the PCs, to avoid disruption and generate income towards the purchase of new equipment.
- The PC plan for the marketing department should be part of the office information–processing strategy and not a stand–alone decision; in the past this has often led to the piecemeal purchase of a high–quality photocopier, faster printer or a new PC, but a failure to automate the whole process. An uncoordinated approach to IT in the marketing department will predictably lead to a failure to deliver efficiency and productivity gains.

For IT to bring about sustained gains in marketing productivity, it is important that the equipment acquired, workplace design and staff training plans have an impact in terms of improved marketing throughout the organization, allowing people to concentrate on value–added duties such as product development, customer relations and retention of existing customers.

KEY ISSUES

- With increased quantities of data and information available to marketing decision–makers, a distinction has to be made between data and knowledge, and between IT and information.
- Interactive marketing via the Internet has created a form of continuing dialogue with the customer that is not subject to the traditional promotion lag. Time and effort in marketing and selling is freed–up; more importantly, cybermarketing provides an opportunity to interactively reach the home–shopping customer.
- Home Internet usage has not yet achieved the status of a universal marketing medium; ownership is still concentrated in the USA and the Scandinavian states with usage currently skewed in narrow demographic terms to males between 25 and 35.
- Developing an ongoing dialogue and sharing information with current and potential customers are the two main benefits of Internet marketing; but the cybermarketing tool must be integrated into other aspects of the marketing activity and not become a stand–alone, esoteric corporate initiative.
- The presence of a corporate Internet site *per se* will not sell products or services; customers have to be lured to the company's cyberspace site with compelling information about their needs – ie generic and product–specific information.
- The combined impact of (1) growth in multicultural societies, rendering retail activities more localized, and (2) the unselective thrust of much contemporary marketing, resulting in wasted resources, has created the need for better profiling of the customer; much of the information about the customer is stored on dispersed corporate databases.
- Companies must distinguish between valued–customers – frequent, high–value purchasers – and value–customers – who purchase items selectively; marketing programmes should be more discriminating in reaching both categories.
- Databases and data–warehousing techniques will help to more accurately identify and profile the customer, but they will not persuade the customer to visit the store; nor will they replace the personal selling role so essential for many customers in guiding them to the ultimate choice of product.

- The IT investment has to be managed better to obtain cost–effective and value–added marketing results; the five–year cost of networked PC ownership can be in excess of $40,000 and the more fragmented the IT configuration in the marketing operation, the higher the costs.
- The acid test of IT investments in equipment, workplace design and training, must be measured in terms of improved marketing: allowing staff to concentrate on value–added duties like product development, customer relations and retention of the valuable customer.

BIBLIOGRAPHY

G Black, 'Less junk mail on the doormat', *Financial Times* (4 September 1996)

D Bradshaw, 'Technology in the office', *Financial Times* (21 October 1989)

R Bray, 'Know your customer base', *Financial Times* (11 April 1996)

C Brown–Humes, 'Warning over on–line shopping', *Financial Times* (12 August 1996)

N Buckley, 'Check out the television', *Financial Times* (19–20 August 1995)

J Bullmore, 'Advertising costs half as much as you think it does... but do you know which half?', Institute of Practitioners in Advertising

C Coughlan, 'The internet and cybermarketing part II', *MII News* (June 1996)

S Coutou, 'Wired up for future growth', *Offshore Financial Review* (June 1996)

N Denton, 'Advertisers eyeball the net', *Financial Times* (17 March 1997)

The Economist, 'A survey of electronic commerce' (10 May 1997)

The Economist, 'A survey of travel & tourism' (10 January 1998)

Financial Times, 'Doing business on–line', Financial Times/.net the Internet magazine (December 1996)

W Fletcher, 'Net facts burst ads bubble', *Financial Times* (7 October 1996)

V Griffith, 'Customers on target', *Financial Times* (18 August 1995)

V Griffith, 'Madison Ave ad agencies eye modem era', *Financial Times* (22 April 1996)

V Griffith, 'Era of ads for your eyes only', *Financial Times* (20 May 1996)

V Griffith, 'Taking risks with d–mail', *Financial Times* (24 May 1996)

F Hannigan, 'The year of electronic commerce', *Irish Marketing Journal* (January 1998)

S Hirel, 'La Frances'équipe lentement', *Le Figaro* (14 August 1996)

P Hollinger, 'Online shopping ready for take–off', Financial Times (20 January 1998) V Houlder, 'Database mining', *Financial Times* (28 November 1995)

V Houlder, 'Warehouse parties', *Financial Times* (23 October 1996)

V Houlder, 'A blossoming relationship', *Financial Times* (28 July 1997)

V Houlder, 'Fear and enterprise on the net', *Financial Times* (20 May 1998)

IriS network (International Research Institutes), 'Business and consumer attitudes to the internet' (1997)

Irish Marketing Journal, 'Internet still has a long way to go' (September 1996)

Irish Marketing Journal, 'The advance of the internet now seems unstoppable' (January 1998)

L Kehoe, 'The armchair shopper', *Financial Times* (22 October 1994)

L Kehoe, 'Amelio's Apple turnover', *Financial Times* (17 May 1996)

L Kehoe, 'High streets in hyperspace', *Financial Times* (18–19 April 1998)

L Kehoe, 'Apple chief has Dell in his sights', *Financial Times* (14 November 1998)

Management Accounting, 'Ineffective IT identified as a problem for marketing' (January 1998)

J McCune, 'House of data', *AMA Management Review* (March 1997)

L Miller, 'Net surfers becoming more mainstream, survey says', *USA Today* (15 August 1996)

R Newing, 'How IT helps to maximize sales', *Financial Times* (5 November 1997)

OECD, 'Electronic Commerce', OECD Policy Brief, 1 (1997)

C Romano, 'The new gold rush?', *AMA Management Review* (November 1995)

R Snoddy, 'Many big companies fail to invest in electronic marketing' (reporting on Harris Research for KPMG), *Financial Times* (1 October 1996)

P Taylor, 'Spotlight on ownership costs', *Financial Times* (1 November 1995)

P Taylor, 'Publishers to charge web users', *Financial Times* (29 December 1997)

P Williams, 'Marketing in cyberspace', *AMA Marketing Forum* (September 1996)

M Wiltshire, 'Technology still "widely misunderstood" – companies' efforts hampered by ineffective IT systems', *Financial Times* (5 November 1997)

P Wolfraim, 'Creating order from chaos', *AMA Management Review* (March 1996)

B Ziegler, 'Will Cyber–advertisers pay for attention?', *The Wall Street Journal* (15–16 November 1996)

7

REDEFINING
THE MARKETING ROLE

For most of the past four decades, corporate heads have relied on the survival kit pronounced by Professor Theodore Levitt of the Harvard Business School back in the 1960s: survival depends on doing everything necessary to satisfy the customer, and marketing is the one and only true way to achieve this enlightened objective. Marketing was to become one of the most disarmingly attractive concepts to sweep the corridors of corporations around the globe. Definitions and functional focus – sometimes inseparable – differed depending on the industry, but invariably relied on variations on the customer theme: 'customer satisfaction', 'customer needs', 'customer service', 'customer culture' *et al.* became the marketing buzzwords. Such definitions were so obsessed with the notion of the customer that little mention was made of profits. Conceptually, and in practice, the quest to satisfy the customer at any cost, or without knowledge of the real costs, has somehow lost touch with the ultimate corporate objective: survival, as measured by profitability and liquidity.

Forty years on, consumer goods companies now find themselves operating in a very different environment from that of the 1960s, with multiple partners in the value-chain playing a role in attracting the customers' attention and loyalty.

The new challenges facing traditional marketing departments today involve private labels/own-brands, big and increasingly influential retailing groups and a fickle customer, increasingly ready to change brands if not satisfied. Marketers have not always responded with the appropriate actions in the marketplace: product-line extensions instead of innovative products, new market segments increasingly more expensive to serve and technology which reaches only a fragment of the potential audience.

In the eyes of many experts, marketing seems to be in a mid-life crisis. The reasons, some of which have already been discussed in previous chapters, can be attributed to eight main factors.

- The use of outdated tactical concepts of marketing, as defined in terms of the '4 Ps' – product, promotion, place and price.
- A marketing role that remains synonymous with selling and promotion rather than an integral and holistic customer-oriented policy to be followed by all parts of the organization.
- A marketing function that tends to be a stand-alone function with limited integration with other parts of the organization.
- Corporate cultures obsessed with cost reduction rather than removing activities and tasks not adding value in delivering customer satisfaction.
- Wasteful diversion of energy and resources, due to:

– Internal customers
– Market diversification
– Product/service proliferation.

- Misguided acquisitions and the failure to productively integrate best practices in marketing.
- Poor tracking and inaccurate allocation of marketing-related costs.
- Changing customer perceptions and demographics.

THE '4 PS' REDEFINED

Product

Product range – is it optimal?
The marketing concept, based on the '4 P' – designated tactical thrust – product, promotion, place and price – may need to be reappraised to determine if it works from the customer's perspective, rather than in terms of its original conception based on market conditions of a different era. The product policy pursued by many corporations world-wide provides a starting point. Instead of developing truly innovative products for markets that are fragmenting and ageing, companies are pursuing more product-line extensions. Marketers argue that more products are needed for a growing segmented market. The reality is that as markets fragment and become more prosperous there is a limit to how many bars or varieties of chocolate the consumer will wish to eat, how many times a week she will wash her hair, how many electrical appliances a household needs.

International brand manufacturers are also discovering that

selling a wide range of products can add complexities at all levels in the organization. Electrolux, the Swedish household appliances group, found that carrying a multitude of brands burdened it with a significantly higher working capital inefficiency ratio compared to its competitors like Whirlpool. Maintaining many brands not only led to production complexities due to production overlap, but also inflated the marketing costs. Two months after Gil Amelio took over at Apple Computer, he remarked that the company 'had tried to do too much... too many products, too many programs, too much of everything – except invest in the future'. Matsushita, the world's largest consumer electronics group, noted that the constant expansion of its product range had led to excessive investment in existing product ranges, mirroring the practices of other Japanese electronics manufacturers. At one stage, there were 220 types of TV and 62 types of VCR across the industry, but only 10 per cent of these sold. Matsushita finally began to pay attention to what the customer was saying when it found that they did not want 20 buttons on a VCR.

Product offerings were not the only area of expansion in the marketing war chest; the other associated elements of the '4 Ps' also suffered from the same desire to proliferate. Procter & Gamble, in response to greater competition, retailer consolidation and fewer product innovations, recently took stock of its situation in the USA: the company implemented some 55 price changes a day across 110 brands, offered 440 promotions a year, and proposed constant amendments to package size, colour and contents. Many companies are discovering that attempts to over-extend the '4 Ps' is leading to consumer confusion and strained relations with the retail trade. The longer-term risks of such a policy are now dawning on corporations and leading to a fundamental rethinking of marketing policy. Nine factors in particular provoked a re-appraisal of the '4 Ps'.

- ■ The female consumer. The average consumer for a wide range of household products is frequently a female who spends just 21 minutes to get through her shopping. She purchases an average of 18 items, out of a choice of 30,000-40,000 offerings. Studies show that she has less time to wander around the store – down 25 per cent from the early 1990s. More frequently than not, she does not even check the bill; she goes for the same product, at the same price that she expects to find in the same aisle, week in, week out. Yet, many consumer product companies in the past decade have ignored these trends, preferring to launch a series of variations of existing successful products via line extensions.

■ Confused strategic thrust. Retailers, faced with ever-increasing ranges of products and extensions, cannot stock everything. In 1980 a typical supermarket stocked 10,000 items; today the figure is about 30,000 according to the Chatham House Forum 1997 Report. Meanwhile, marketing people remain circumspect about removing any existing items. The result is a confused strategic thrust for each product at sales staff level and inevitable stockouts of the consumers' preferred size and flavour. Customer disaffection, brand zapping or the quest for an all-purpose product occurs.

■ Product-line extension. Over the 1980s, marketing people were quick to notice that new product development was a protracted process with unpredictable results. This was reinforced by the reality that only one in five new products launched in the USA lasted longer than one year on the market. Pressure from the shareholder community for more 'shareholder value' and improved quarterly earnings led to less emphasis on new product development, requiring investments in long-term R & D and fixed assets. The development time and costs associated with product-line extensions was seen as an easier route to profitability. This policy, however, overlooked one salient fact: the customers show an increasing interest in more than just the initial purchase transaction and are more concerned about their total experience of product ownership over time. Satisfaction with the entire ownership experience is important because happy customers are loyal customers. This relationship weakens as brand extensions are introduced, thereby diluting its image and that of the company.

■ Cost management. Improved cost management techniques such as ABC (see Chapter 4) brought the hidden cost nature of product proliferation policies to the surface.

■ Increased customization. Increased customization of products for multiple market segments leads to dilution of the brand image and less than effective impact in terms of marketing effort and resources.

■ Administrative and support costs. Additional products result in growth in administrative and marketing support costs for promotion, logistics, accounts receivable effort and stock handling.

- Cross-subsidization. High-volume sales items tend to cross-subsidize the slow-moving items – a feature not recognized under the traditional cost-accounting systems, which allocate overheads to products based on their pro-rata sales.
- Costs of complexity. Aside from the overall increased levels of complexity of handling 20 items instead of five, certain products may inherently be more complex to manufacture, store, quality control and sell; corporations rarely consider the costs of complexity arising from the costs to sell and serve, and the incremental costs of adding additional products to the range.
- Dilution of earnings. It costs one-fifth to one-sixth as much to retain a customer as it does to acquire a new one. Adding new customers and additional products, without knowledge of the incremental costs and potential revenues, will lead to ultimate dilution of earnings resulting from the onerous cost burden to be absorbed.

A re-appraisal of the product range, the customer base and '4 Ps'

Managing the 'customer ownership experience' better requires a more balanced sense of flexibility and focus in building a product policy *vis-à-vis* the customer base and a more precise mix of the '4 Ps'. Instead of simply extending elements and components to existing marketing policies, some consideration has to be given to the basics of where the company is now, and where it goes from here.

Marketing needs to adopt a policy of preventive care according to the management guru, Peter Drucker, who warned that companies must remain alert and be capable of rapidly changing themselves by taking proactive action with regard to the marketplace. The preventive measures are encapsulated in Drucker's notions of abandonment and nonconsumers.

- Abandonment calls for the marketing department to challenge every three years, each product, service, promotional activity and every distribution channel with the question: If the company wasn't in it already, would it be going into it now? This forces management to test previous assumptions about the products' core values, suitability for current consumer needs, whether the promotional activities are working – in short, is the company putting more effort into 'doing things right' rather than 'doing the right things'? This allows for:

- the removal of unnecessary variations with product lines in certain markets to make it easier for customers to understand the choice on the shelves
- the discontinuing of inappropriate promotional vehicles like 'buy one, get one free', targeted at the wrong people – ie wealthier customers who could afford to buy in bulk
- the consolidation of individual customer-service structures across markets that are simply no longer viable on a multiple-market basis
- the rationalization of pricing policy by reducing the multitude of pricing lists – ie by reducing them from, for instance, 34 to three; this also facilitates electronic order-taking, thereby cutting order errors significantly
- freeing-up HQ from excessive paperwork associated with supervision, controls, mandates, analysis, etc.

■ The product rationalization policy needs to also look at the associated administrative burdens of the corporate promotion and pricing procedures: the greater the intensity and diversity of the promotional and pricing activities, the greater the administrative burden at HQ, and amongst the sales staff in the field. One major consumer products' company, who had traditionally based its marketing thrust on bigger and better promotions to move cases of diapers, pet food and shampoo through the trade, discovered the magnitude of its administrative burdens: paperwork, both in the field and at HQ, was at nightmare proportions. Simple orders placed by retailers at $100 were shipped by the supplier at $128, leading to multiple errors on orders in one out of four transactions. The company was forced to deploy an *ad hoc* 150-staff unit just to deal with 30,000 orders a month manually, at a cost of $60 per order.

■ Streamlining of the product lines must be balanced with another trend in contemporary markets: an ever-shorter product life-cycle. This puts the marketing and engineering teams under great pressure to design and devise an appropriate marketing programme. This should not be an ephemeral effort every few years, but rather a consistently forward-looking culture, to identify customer requirements with great precision. Getting the product wrong for the market segment – over-specified or under-specified – results in missed opportunities.

■ The second imperative is to look at the customer base – both current and future – for opportunities to rationalize, attract new clientele and consolidate.

■ Nonconsumers. Drucker suggests examining what goes on outside the company, and, in particular, to get to grips with the nonconsumers. As he put it

> the first signs of fundamental change rarely appear within one's own organization or among one's own customers. Almost always they show up first among one's noncustomers.

The most compelling example of this is the emergence of the baby-boomer two-earner household, where the female is a 'working partner' and clearly has less time to shop than before, as we saw above. Price has proven not to be the essential factor in attracting customers in this group; time is the primary consideration. Many retail groups failed to recognize these phenomena because they were focused on their own current customers. Convenient store layouts, fast-track checkouts, a smaller but more coherent product range, on-line shopping facilities, home deliveries, etc were of more interest to this group than offering shoppers a bewildering amount of choice of 50,000 different items and expecting the consumer to shop the entire mega-store to find the relatively few items on their shopping list. Retailers have learned that being customer-driven is simply not sufficient; the stores also had to be market-driven.

The customer – a valuable asset or a dog?

The balancing act doesn't end there; a deeper analysis of the current customer base is required to eliminate redundancy and concentrate resources on value-added customers. The key question marketing heads should be asking is: Should the company go for the mass-customer market or be more selective? Many marketing experts now acknowledge that not all customers are equally valuable. Borrowing a quadrant from the Boston Consulting Group's much-respected 2x2 matrix, every company has a standard customer portfolio profile: some customers are cash cows, a few are stars, many are question marks; too many are dogs that end up costing companies far more money than they are worth, suggesting that they should not be encouraged.

Today, few companies can afford the luxury of considering everyone as an existing or potential customer. Like any asset, rigorous analysis must be employed to ensure a decent return on the investment in the acquisition, development and retention of customers. The aim is to go for the most valuable, and thus most profitable, customers. As a starting point it is worth remembering that the old axiom still holds true: 80 per cent of sales arise from 20 per cent of customers. The most attractive customers are those who demonstrate a relatively high degree of preference for the company's products on a sustainable basis. Conversely, the existence of customers attracted by the company's products but who consume inordinate marketing resources without concomitant results over a sustainable timeframe are likely to be low profit-generating customers. A case in point are the cellular telephone companies, many of whom found that mass-customer-based marketing programmes offering free telephones and calling time did little to entice the right kind of customer; many turned out to be low-usage, transient customers and thus unprofitable in the long term.

Low usage is not the only factor contributing to low-profitable customers; a range of 'customer-sustaining activities' managed by different parts of the organization can also dilute the value of an otherwise profitable customer segment: frequent inquiries, small, fragmented orders, special packaging instructions, lengthy payment delays, onerous accounts receivable effort, extensive customization of products and customer services can all provoke different cost patterns, not necessarily recouped in the final price to the customer.

To summarize, identifying the core profitable customers can be assisted by addressing three inter-related questions.

- Which of the company's customers spend the most money on the products, pay their bills on time, require less 'servicing' and seem to be keen on a stable perennial relationship with the company?
- From surveys and casual discussions, which of the company's customers articulate the greatest value on what the company offers? Typically, those closest to the customer, like salespeople, are best positioned to give an opinion on such issues.
- Which categories are worth more in revenue terms to the company than to competitors? Some customers may justify additional effort and investment than others, but obsession with zero defections can lead companies to heavy investment in aggressive promotional effort that is simply disproportionate to the value of the customers' business.

Ongoing development of customers' business
Customer relations can be misdirected if it is not focused on the opportunity to consolidate business with profitable customers who are prepared to stay with the company for a long run. Customers can evolve from being regular and loyal customers to being profitable ones if the company can entice them to shift their buying behaviour to higher margin products. Techniques include cross-selling which has been skilfully used by financial service companies who market credit-card facilities and use their customer data-base to build programmes to entice their current customers to higher-value services such as tourism, investment and life insurance. Customer consolidation can also be productively implemented on the basis of market concentration, thereby minimizing resource wastage in marketing effort and time. One French bakery group selling a range of baguettes, oatmeal bread and patisseries by special delivery each day to customer's homes, chooses the site of their stores on the basis of where its potential growth customers are. When the group identifies a geographic cluster of regular buyers, it then considers that location for a retail store. As described in Chapter 6, frequent shopper discount cards are also used at checkouts by some stores to track customers' buying preferences and habits, thereby providing a more accurate insight into those worth cultivating. The key implication here is that marketing policy can be more profitably determined when:

■ the customer base is more sharply defined
■ marketing activities are subject of less wastage because the company is, in principle, reaching only those interested in the product
■ customer defection can be identified and remedied more promptly
■ product and promotional proliferation can be kept to measurable limits – ie the customer either responds positively or does not.

Retain the existing customer – it costs less!
Clearly, marketing efforts and resources should be earmarked to retain the most profitable customers – those who cost less to serve, are repeat buyers and who evolve to higher margin offerings. The challenge is not only in identifying them, but also retaining their business. It is estimated that US corporations lose half

their customers every five years, and because every new customer costs money to acquire, the cashflows – and, ultimately, the
profits – suffer in the interim period while the company struggles
to build long-term loyalty. This new customer cycle can be long
and costly. The more the perennial nature of the customers' relationship with the company, the more that customer is worth in
terms of future revenue streams. Simply put, long-term customers
buy more, absorb less sales' staff time and require less input from
corporate support services, are less price-sensitive and also influence others to try the product. From the financial perspective,
they do not incur costs for start-up or acquisition.

This does not imply that losing a customer justifies aggressive
customer recovery programmes; over-reliance on customer retention can often be at the expense of necessary investments in
developing replacement customer bases. Commodity-type products and services requiring inordinate customer-service input can
be sub-optimal when compared to targeting faster-growing customer segments linked to value-added services offered by the
company.

Retaining 80 per cent of the core profitable customer base is a
realistic and measurable objective for all marketing operations.
Yet, few marketing departments consider developing an ongoing
mechanism to ensure that the key people dealing with customers
– and not necessarily only in marketing – are permanently monitoring outside events, habits, preferences and other features that
could trigger off defections. One US insurance company has set up
an early-warning system to detect any internal or external event
that could lead to defection with the help of its life-stage segment
analysis. Its data-base profiles each customer and alerts management to future events – such as the arrival of a new child, the
spouse returning to work, children reaching driving age, etc-
thereby enabling the company to identify potential reasons for
defection (or new opportunities) early and develop responses.
The US insurance company cited above boasts a customer defection rate of less than 2 per cent per year.

This task will not be made easy if staff are indulging in unproductive diversions in-house in pursuit of satisfying the 'internal
customer' rather than outside customers. The focus on 'internal
customers' – ie support services, reporting requirements, etc-
diverts attention away from the people who assure future cashflows – the outside customer. Obsession with efficiency in deliver-

ing reports and professional services to various units of the organization renders internal services oblivious to external customer concerns. Marshalling the energy and skills of HRM, MIS, legal affairs, etc into ways directly impacting on the external customer is a must. One European airline, CEO, in an attempt to get staff refocused on customers, assigned every employee the task of redefining his or her job, linked to attracting and retaining the business traveller.

However, innovation is still an imperative... look a customer ahead

Differentiating one's self from the other companies in the market selling commodity-type products requires retaining the loyal and profitable customers with the appropriate mix of products and service. However, no customer lasts forever. Demographics, technological developments and fragmentation of markets will inevitably lead to a certain proportion of customers disappearing from the company's portfolio each year. The financial services industries, such as banks and insurance companies, are only too aware of the effects of ageing of its customer base: when a customer dies, valuable business is lost. There is thus an imperative to continually 'look a customer ahead'. This should not be part of an isolated burst of activity every couple of years, but an integral and continuous part of marketing plans, to be followed by staff at all levels in the organization.

Companies that prepare themselves for obsolescence, in terms of products and customer services offered, and even anticipating obsolescence of the market itself, will be better equipped to handle this task. This requires freeing-up of staff from administrative work and putting them at the customers' disposal to listen for echoes of imminent change in the marketplace. One of Germany's largest banks developed a plan aimed at empowering staff to build a better understanding of customers. Under its *Projekt Kundennahe* (getting closer to the customers), it called for visits of board members to branches throughout the country, and training for staff to give financial advice to customers and persuade them to buy a wider range of products. The company insists that everyone, including senior staff, be out in the field regularly – interviewing customers, observing their investment habits and assumptions, jointly solving problems that previously constituted impediments, and sharing ideas and information back at the local branches. The bank restructured branch networks throughout Germany by shifting administrative work such as processing customer loans to special centres and re-deploying staff to advise customers. Every customer contact thus becomes a sales contact and a forward listening post to monitor changing conditions in the market.

Promotion

Promotion – a dispersed tool

With markets ageing faster and subject to more fragmentation because of greater choice of channels, companies are increasingly concerned that TV advertising is not as effective a tool as in the past. Advertisers have spent millions chasing the much-prized young and high-income groups. The trend is shifting towards older and, what some media experts describe as, 'more downmarket' audiences, viewing what they regard as a declining level of quality TV programmes. While reaching mass markets remains feasible, it is increasingly difficult to reach more niche groups, and the multitude of channels adds additional complexity. Now big advertising spenders amongst the consumer product manufacturers are examining individual programmes, like TV quizzes and soap operas, with a view to assessing if they fit its quality criteria, and correspond to the right setting and audiences for its products. Some companies have pursued this approach by investing funds in the production, in return for sponsoring the programme, which offers the opportunity to plug its brand name or logo.

Advertising has undergone a major shift in the past decade in response to more demanding clients, the growth in new media and escalating promotional costs, the effects of which are beginning to impact on the way this tool is employed in the marketing mix. Five issues are relevant here.

■ Space buying is no longer restricted to traditional TV. A plethora of advertising media now exist, including television in multiple terrestrial, orbital, analogue and digital forms, journals and magazines catering for every hobby and life-style theme, and billboards and bus shelters. Nevertheless, TV still remains the prime source of information and entertainment in the USA (see Table 7.1), while newspaper circulation has retained credible proportions in the Scandanavian states, Japan, Hong Kong and South Korea (see Table 7.2).

Table 7.1 *Who watches TV in USA: still a force in media selection?*
64 per cent of TV households subscribe to cable TV

- Average TV household receives 41 channels, including broadcast and cable
- Average TV household views 7 hours and 20 minutes per day
- 72 per cent of Americans rely on TV as their primary news source, and 51 per cent cite TV as the most believable news source.

Source: NAB Library & Information Centre (1997).

Table 7.2 *Newspaper circulation: daily circulation per 1,000 inhabitants (1993)*

Australia	258	Austria	472
Belgium	321	Canada	189
China	23	Denmark	365
Finland	473	France	237
Germany	317	Greece	156
Hong Kong	719	India	31
Ireland	170	Israel	281
Italy	105	Japan	576
South Korea	404	Mexico	113
Netherlands	334	New Zealand	297
Norway	607	Portugal	41
Russia	267	Spain	104
Sweden	483	Switzerland	409
UK	351	USA	228

Source: The IMD World Competitiveness Yearbook (1997).

Table 7.3 *Global advertising expenditure forecasts: main media: TV, print, radio, cinema, outdoor ($billion at current prices)*

	1996	1997	1998	1999
North America	105	110	115	120
Europe	82	86	92	97
Asia/Pacific	78	85	93	102
Latin America	21	23	26	30
Other	6	6	7	8

Source: Zenith Media (London).

■ Economies of scale have improved as a result of the mega mergers of media companies on a world-wide scale. The more space that is purchased, the better the rates obtained for advertisers. Media planning and media buying is now a specialized expertise in itself, which can be carried out on a global scale by pan-European media firms out of London or Paris with savings up to 10 per cent of the advertising budget.

■ Promoting one name and one image across multiple markets is increasingly seen as being desirable, but requires a standard approach from the TV commercial right down to the salesperson's handbook in the showroom. Companies are finding that this is not always best achieved by having 30 separate agencies, all with their own objectives. Using one agency also offers the opportunity to negotiate lower fees because there are fewer fixed costs associated with one agency rather than 30.

■ Retailers are becoming more adept at analysing the impact of advertising on sales. Assisted by bar-coding, stock control and accelerated turnover, the speed and accuracy with which ad campaigns can be assessed has improved: if the checkouts fail to register the expected sales, retailers quickly change their promotional mix.

■ Consumer product manufacturers have also improved their knowledge of advertising effectiveness with the help of more accurate and prompt sales audits, continuous consumer purchase panels (now possible over the Internet), awareness tracking studies and the introduction of sophisticated IT techniques. Information Age technologies now reveal precise details about individuals, allowing for:

– greater precision of the target market for the brand
– clustering them into segments
– facilitating the creation of appropriately targeted messages
– driving the selection of the most appropriate media
– measuring the effects of specific advertisements.

High cost of sustaining brands

For mainstream brands in developed economies, it is becoming increasingly costly for companies to maintain and 'refresh' existing product lines. According to the marketing consultancy Added Value, the average cost of maintaining a top-ten brand in the mid-1990s was about 7 per cent of sales; for the market followers, promotional and advertising expenditures represented 10 per cent of sales. These figures underline the necessity of re-appraising the company's product portfolios in relation to promotional and advertising support that is needed in the future to simply sustain the current market position. It is clear that products that have not attained critical mass in their respective markets will have high ratios of promotional and advertising expenditure to sales.

Responses to increased promotional cost pressure have varied, but some companies have developed strategies to make more effective use of budgets by:

- producing TV commercials that consistently feature the corporate name, thereby re-allocating the advertising budget evenly across all brands
- employing an umbrella branding policy whereby all the company's brand advertising is devised to enhance the profile of its various sub-brands
- shifting marketing expenditures into direct marketing, by using data warehousing techniques to target the customer more precisely.

The sales function – the Cinderella of marketing

The role of the salesman has long been associated with Arthur Miller's 'smile and shoe shine' image (see below), representing the human side of the marketing operation to outside clients. Past attempts to match value with costs of such deployments have not always been easy to measure. Compounding this is the anecdotal evidence showing how neglected salesforces have been in many corporate marketing environments. Yet research shows that this neglect cannot be sustained by corporations for much longer.

- The average annual cost of a salesperson in the UK is just below £50,000. Many companies employ salesforces that cost more than their annual advertising expenditure. More revealing is the proportion of costs attributed to the sales function in terms of management, support, travel and expenses: over 50 per cent of the total cost.
- Salespeople's time is not always spent on handling anything remotely associated with the customer: 35 per cent of time was spent on travelling, 20 per cent on administration and 14 per cent on meetings; only 6 per cent of time was actually devoted to selling. A study carried out by Matsushita, the Japanese consumer electronics company, revealed that only

20 per cent of working hours put in by marketing staff were directly related to customers' business; much work, not only at HQ but among group companies, was being duplicated.

Part of the problem lies in the poor definition of tasks, and the failure to exploit the untapped knowledge of the salespeople. This is best exemplified by the case of one maritime transport company, who after examining a customer satisfaction survey, drew the conclusion that its clients were not satisfied. Salespeople were sent out to spread cheer and re-cultivate relationships. Despite such efforts, the company continued to lose clients, until it discovered that a low-cost, innovative service offered by a competitor was the real issue, not dissatisfaction. The company had dispatched the salesforce to fix the wrong problem and waste time that should have been spent on service development. More worryingly, the salespeoples' valuable intimate knowledge of the customers had not been exploited.

Shifting the sales function out of the realm of its Cinderella association with marketing requires a fundamental revision of the relationship between salespeople and customers. Multicountry studies show that this can be achieved by converting the salespeople into the strategic relationship-builder, business consultant and long-term partner *vis-à-vis* the customer.

- This could commence with a policy of differentiating levels of responsibility required to handle big customers and small customers. Here the 80/20 rule is of importance: for many companies, 80 per cent of its business is shared among 20 per cent of its customers. It makes little financial sense to chase all customers, dissipating energy and resources and, as a result, failing to meet customer requirements. The accounts of important customers should normally need a higher level of servicing than smaller accounts.
- Building closer relationships with key large-account customers requires a broader range of skills than those of the Lone Ranger type of salesman epitomized in Arthur Miller's book *Death of a Salesman*. Extravert personality traits and willingness to work may not be enough. These traits must be supplemented with analytical skills and customer problem-solving capacities. This implies an interactive role with other people in the organization to provide an integrated service, from defining the needs of the customer right through to post-cus-

tomer servicing. One leading high-tech company uses its sales-force in a consultative selling role by stationing technicians in customer plants. This offers an opportunity to work more closely with clients to determine problems and identify oppor-tunities. The sales technicians, which it calls 'implants', work closely with the customers' engineers in place to provide advice on the company's high-tech products and improve pro-duction efficiency, as part of the sales package. To some extent, this has eliminated the need for traditional sales calls as they can readily alert the marketing department to market opportunities as they evolve. Aside from obtaining a better knowledge of the customers' needs, this approach also mini-mizes or even abolishes the order-processing function back at HQ as orders can be channelled and processed via the techni-cians.

- The salesperson's role is seen as being more effective when structured vertically within the organization. Instead of seven different representatives, each with a specific line, assigned to make separate sales calls on one retailer, some companies have opted for teams, consisting of salespeople and experts in market research, logistics, shelf management and manufactur-ing. The salesperson, no longer being subject to different poli-cies dictated by HQ, would deal with one retailer for a range of products and be capable of planning delivery schedules syn-chronized in terms only of what is needed, based on cash-reg-ister data of what quantities of certain products have been sold. The salesperson can then spend more time fine-tuning the retail customers' needs, avoiding anticipated stockouts and devising promotions that local shoppers like.

- Technology has created new opportunities to build relation-ships with customers at lower costs. One manifestation of this is the telesales and call centres approach, which have over-taken the traditional salesforce function. Sales outlets and other overheads can be dramatically slashed in the process. Car insurance and banking services now offer direct telecom-munications with the customer without the need for branch networks; the customer conceivably benefits with lower rates for service provision. But telesales systems can be seriously handicapped if the staff remain poorly trained. Little attention has been paid to the important aspects of recruitment, selec-tion and training for this specific role, which requires specialized skills. The salesperson who interfaces with the customer over the phone is frequently the only link with the company and on whom they will judge the price and quality of the service they receive. Often the product and the service are inseparable, making it more vital to select the right 'fit' for the role.

- IT can also affect the speed that salespeople can deliver value to customers. In the past, many salespeople would take down information at the customer's plant or store, return to the office, consult with engineers, production, logistics, etc and get price information from the finance people, before returning to the client with a quote. Now, salespeople can provide a quote while sitting in the customer's office. In more sophisticated IT applications, salespeople not only have laptops but the computer can configure complex products 'customized' to the customer's requirements, on the spot.

- The performance assessment system for salespeople should go beyond traditional volume and revenue sales targets achieved to embrace more quantifiable measures that the company might consider are important for sustainable profitable growth. Examples could include: How many orders were delivered on time? What percentage of bills is accurate? Have the customers paid their bills promptly?

- As key people with intimate knowledge of the customer, salespeople also play a valuable role in gathering market intelligence and scanning opportunities and potential problems. Undertaking this extended role requires that the salespeople spend more time preparing for their customer calls. Increasingly, they are being called upon to know more about, and collect information on, the marketplace, industry and their customers, in a manner that they may not have done systematically in the past. Structuring the sales operation vertically to facilitate this thrust is essential, in order for each salesperson to be assigned a single speciality sector, such as aeronautics, insurance or the public sector.

- With companies focusing on growth and creating more market-focused organizations, the orientation is now on building sustainable growth by putting more emphasis on how companies sell their products. All this is happening at a time when companies are realizing – somewhat belatedly – that some customers are more valuable than others. This implies re-deploying salespeople on key accounts, creating real selling teams, and having senior management spend less time behind their desks and more in the field – more often. Many companies have reduced the overall size of their salesforce, turning over less profitable customers to telemarketing departments.

Place

The distribution environment – a more cluttered arena
The third element of the infamous '4 Ps', place – designating the distribution strategy used by the company – is a more complex and cluttered arena today than in the post-war years. The increased clout of the retail trade in developed economies has led to mega-store groups taking the forefront in attracting customers with lower prices, loyalty cards, own-brands, home delivery and longer opening hours. Hypermarket and supermarket stores now dominate the retail structure in most European states except Italy. They have consistently generated annual rates of sales growth of 6 per cent since the early 1990s; however, with planning requirements tightening across the EU, the growth of discounters, the use of increasingly sophisticated information technology (ie electronic data interchange (EDI) and data warehousing, see Chapter 6) and the growth of home shopping, albeit at an embryonic stage, the mega-groups are having to re-assess their strategies to compete.

The real losers in this retail battle have been the small high-street retailers and grocers. Between 1975 and 1990, the number of grocery stores in the UK halved while the average size of the top five retailers has doubled. Some retail categories have done better than others by being more focused; many privately-owned clothes chains in the UK have achieved return of capital increases that overshadowed quoted competitors and their peers on mainland Europe: between 45 and 60 per cent per year. Success amongst these chains has been attributed to tight financial controls and a marketing thrust based on relatively few brands and a clear target market.

The enhanced fortunes of the mega-groups has been accompanied by concomitant growth of own-brand packaged food and groceries' items, which has seen its share boosted to more than 30 per cent in the period. In Europe, own-brand sales have grown over five years by an average of 7.5 per cent a year at present prices, compared with 3.4 per cent for overall retail sales growth. In the USA, in the highly competitive packaged food sector, own-brands have shot up from 20 per cent of the market in 1990 to just under 25 per cent by 1994. Evidence provided by McKinsey Consultants suggests that these trends will continue to grow, despite marginal penetration in some EU states such as Portugal, Norway, Spain and Italy.

Discount stores, situated in urbanized street-corner locations and run with lean staff resources, have also presented another threat to producers: they offer only fast-moving items and own-label brands devoid of the high added-cost features of national brands such as advertising, logistics and stocking. These retail outlets are expected to represent over 15 per cent of the UK market, while on mainland Europe they already hold sizeable shares of the market in Germany, Belgium and the Scandinavian states. The response of some medium-sized retailers has been to adopt elements of the category killer strategy by specializing in one particular product category. In the short term, strategies of this nature have achieved sufficient volume to cover costs without alienating the customers.

Adding to these challenges, suppliers also face differences in retail influence which vary with region and product category. The UK and US food distribution structures, for instance, are distinguished by a significant structural difference. Food distribution in the UK is dominated by a handful of retailers who promote own-label items, leaving the manufacturers in a distinctly subordinate position. In North America, where retail power is less concentrated, food manufacturers call the shots, even to the extent of devising detailed merchandizing policies with individual stores.

Many large suppliers now recognize that they have not always been winners in this volatile and fast-moving environment. The vast proportion of products are now distributed to stores via central warehouses created by the supermarkets themselves, thus forging a further distance between the producer and the customer. More detailed cost analysis has revealed that the manufacturer's brands are not as profitable as previously thought once the dilutive effect of the 'costs-to-serve' big retail groups is factored in: downward price pressure, more frequent in-store promotions, frequent low-volume deliveries, etc.

In the face of such upheavals, the reaction of many marketing heads has been to launch further variations of past successes in their product range. Line extensions have proven to be a misleading strategy in the long term, faced with customers who have less time to shop and demonstrate less interest in the new products, more attracted by all-purpose and own-brands offered by the retail groups. What customers seem to want is speed and convenience. According to a survey of consumers conducted by Yankelovich Partners in the USA, and sponsored by MasterCard International, 40 per cent of shoppers stated that they would even pay more for an item if the shopping experience were faster and easier. However, consumers are finding that conventional stores simply do not deliver these features on a consistent basis. Investment experts also point to the cultural shift taking place amongst the shopping public in many developed countries. In the 1980s, shopping was considered to be one of the great leisure activities. This has given way to a fashion of discounting the fun element of hauling round the High Streets or driving to an out-of-town shopping centre; many customers now believe that eating out or enjoying a holiday has become a more popular way to spend time – and money.

Reinventing the distribution strategy

Tackling the increased power of the retailer necessitates a fundamental rethinking about distribution policy, that gets results without (1) antagonizing the distributor, (2) alienating the customer and (3) incurring disproportionate costs. Consider the following opportunities and potential risks emerging in the market.

Exploiting synergy. While the problems of communicating with customers may be becoming more complicated for manufacturers, there are signs that the traditional retailing landscape is disintegrating. With supermarkets becoming banks, petrol stations turning into mini-supermarkets, and every conceivable form of home shopping being studied, sales channels are becoming more numerous and finely targeted. Clearly, few manufacturers have any desire to become wholesalers or retailers, but many are convinced that they must investigate and continue to monitor how these channels are evolving to gain a better understanding of fragmented consumer base. Some have taken the plunge.

A case in point is the link-ups between superstores and petrol companies to set up mini-stores on petrol stations. Safeway, the UK store group, forged a joint venture with BP allowing it to set up outlets amongst the oil company's 2,000 service stations, gaining well placed sites for construction of small stores. Another international Oil Company, Royal Dutch/Shell, also examined the feasibility of developing new markets by tapping the potential of having 20 mn people a day calling at the company's 45,000 service stations world-wide.

Re-examine the value of own-branding. The benefits and medium to long-term costs of pursuing an own-brand manufacturing policy need to be re-assessed by marketing heads. Research now shows that own-brand production, often launched as a means of using temporary over-capacity, can result in cannibalizing the company's main brands. Own-brand manufacturing has always had a strong backing from the marketing constituency within organizations, primarily based on arguments that it:

- represents growing markets in most mature developed markets in Europe and North America
- absorbs additional shelf space and thus enhances impulse purchases within-stores
- enables the company to compete on price against competitive brands
- helps to build better relations with the powerful retailing groups
- contributes to discouraging smaller more localized competitors
- supports the consumer surveys on own-brand preferences which point to consumers questioning why they are paying more for the benefit of a brand logo when own-brand versions may be just as good
- requires less promotional and selling effort than national brands.

Problems in handling own-brands over the 1990s have now drawn attention to the harmful effects on the main branded business and the hidden costs associated with managing a parallel line of products. The real economics of own-brands needs to be probed with two key questions: (1) what is the real contribution from own-brands and (2) what fixed costs, both manufacturing and marketing, can be identified and attributed to own-brands?

Closer analysis of the variable costs could reveal incremental manufacturing and distribution activities, the most obvious being changes associated with labelling and packaging per own-brand for each account. Separate stock holdings and associated stock management activities should also be considered in the calculation. On the marketing side, the creation and maintenance of separate sales relationships with retailers will have to be accounted for. Separate sales/marketing operations will undoubtedly lead to conflicts of interest, leading to management time being deployed in resolving conflicts; the proportionate time and cost of a senior marketing person will have to be accounted for in the calculation.

For those companies already engaged in own-brands, more revelations will become apparent when the real profitability of such an approach is calculated, both on the basis of absorption cost (where fixed and variable overhead are charged to each own-brand), and marginal cost (where variable costs are charged to individual own-brands and fixed costs of the period are written-off in full against the aggregate contribution).

Own-brands tend to be more successful, and frequently constitute the only means for head-on competition, when:

- the leading brands charge an excessive price premium, making it difficult to match the competitive rates
- the company manufactures commodity products, where it is difficult to add value
- the company markets a category of basic products characterized by frequent purchase and where consumers are price sensitive
- consumers genuinely see no reason for higher price to be paid for prestige or perceived company quality.

There are no hard and fast rules. McKinsey Consultants, in its review of the status of own-brands in 1993, suggest that companies approach the decision on launching own-brands by being cognisant of the fact that an own-brand does not represent a new segment of the market; it is not an innovative product capable of generating new users, new uses or new occasions of consumption. Being a 'me-too' brand, it succeeds only at the expense of other brands in the market – frequently those manufactured by the same house. Many marketing experts, as a result, view cannibalization of existing national brands as a real threat in the medium to long term, compounded by:

- increased price pressure leading to diminished price position
- diminished share of shelf space
- intensified competition in own-brands from other producers.

Careful choice of distribution partner. The selection of distribution partners – franchisees, retailers and distributors – needs to be more carefully vetted, and has to go beyond volume performance and solid balance sheets. Too often in the past, companies choose their distribution partner in function of its capacity to move the most product, pay receivables on time and the stability of its finances. The distribution partner can be successful in its own right without having to do a good job of satisfying the ultimate customers of the company.

Being in the front-line *vis-à-vis* the customer, the distributor plays an essential role in delivering customer-satisfaction. Not only do distributors control sales, but they also handle delivery, service inquiries and sometimes installation. High-volume sales can be elusive if not accompanied by longer-term sustained maintenance of such customer satisfaction features as the quality of the advice, the receptiveness of the sales staff in the store and the level of service. The Yankelovich Partners' survey in the USA, mentioned above, underlines the disenchantment of four out of ten shoppers who stated that they would even pay more for an item if the shopping experience were faster and easier. The same survey revealed that 62 per cent of the respondents in the past six months had decided to buy something in a store, but then left without a purchase because sales staff were not available.

A motivated sales staff is highly dependent on factors beyond the control of the supplier, which must nevertheless be examined before choosing a partner. One American retail group, in common with the rest of industry, cut jobs to increase profitability. They quickly learned that over-manning was not the main problem: customers complained that poorly trained and uncommitted sales staff could not provide the level of service they had come to expect. The reason was traced back to the reversal of the policy to deploy a 70/30 mix of full to part-time staff to minimize staff costs. The policy of switching to part-time staff proved to be a false economy, provoking a higher level of staff turnover. When management surveyed its staff component, it found that those with the highest staff turnover had the least satisfied customers.

The bottom line is that low satisfaction with the retailer quickly translates into low satisfaction with the manufacturer, which in turn leads to low repurchase loyalty.

Price

Poor costing = misdirected pricing
Of all the elements of the '4 Ps', pricing should ostensibly rank as being the least troublesome as it is usually based on some scientific costing method to determine the price; in reality, devising a pricing policy for many companies is the most troublesome marketing decision. In an article in the *Harvard Business Review* of September 1995, Professor Dolan asserted that pricing represented an area where managers 'feel the most pressure to perform and the least certain that they are doing a good job'.

Yet this should not be the case. Management consultants believe that part of the problem lies with the poor corporate mechanisms for fixing prices, because of the insufficient use of available data in-house. In multiple-product companies, the salespeople frequently hold the responsibility for pricing decisions, but the lack of costing information on each product deters them from increasing prices for fear of losing the sale – even if the outcome results in an increase in profits.

The solution lies in understanding the true cost of each product, encompassing not only the variable elements but also equally the growing fixed expenses. Traditionally, fixed expenses or overheads, a large part of which are marketing-activity-related, have been allocated to a product on the basis of misdirected parameters such as the number of hours worked by staff in the office, on the plant floor or selling in the field. The drawback of the direct labour method is that (1) labour costs are a declining proportion of total costs in most developed countries and (2) the costs allocated bear no relationship to the real activity and effort needed to manufacture and sell each product. Closer examination of the corporate cost base is necessary in order to:

■ build up information on which products generate profits and which lose money
■ avoid inadvertent cross-subsidizing of some products or customers
■ identify those activities/tasks/events in the customer value-chain that simply do not add value
■ adjust the company's pricing structure and focus on its more profitable customers, on the basis of more accurate cost data.

The changing cost environment

Many management accountants are now convinced that truly variable costs will tend to diminish, because the manufacturing element of a product or service has become relentlessly cheaper. By contrast, fixed costs – design, branding and the marketing support elements – become more expensive. In some industries, marketing and manufacturing support costs are growing three times faster than materials and direct labour. The corporate challenge is not so much in tracing costs to products for items like material and labour but more about those costs associated with the dispersed marketing activity.

If cost systems can be re-built to 'mirror' the entire organization, including activities in the marketplace and in the marketing back-office operations, the company should have a better idea of its true cost structures. The marketing overheads can no longer be treated as non-attributable items to a single process, product or system, and left in a pool of costs to be controlled by 'someone else' in the organization; typically, this falls on the financial controller, who indulges in equally judgemental means of controlling and budgeting for many marketing activities through appropriations. If marketing overhead is incorrectly allocated, any one product will bear an overhead allocation in excess of what is warranted, while another may bear an allocation smaller than its actual contribution. Cross-subsidization occurs on a grand scale, which is difficult to change in the absence of more accurate 'activity-driven' costs. The result is poor product costing, which ultimately affects pricing, and profitability.

In addition, poor performers amongst the product range continue to be promoted by the company, cluttering the marketing offerings and adding unnecessary burdens in terms of administrative effort.

Customization – is it priced accurately?

Pursuing a policy of customization of products to respond to multiple market segments should not mean producing variety at any cost, which invariably is not recovered in the final price. Choices for the sake of choice will not inherently create customer value. Customization has to be based on precise costing of the variable and fixed expenses associated with each product made to the customers' specifications, including the incremental costs associated with complexity of delivering one of many elements of the '4 Ps':

tactical advertising campaigns devised for certain cultural or demographic segments, special packaging requirements, accounts receivable effort, in-store promotions, or simply, 'fussy' customers who absorb an inordinate amount of the corporate support services, can all trigger off different cost patterns.

Instead of allocating the marketing overhead to constantly growing and changing product lines, with the intention of developing a standard cost for inventory valuation, marketing heads should be asking the question: 'Where does the money go in the marketing operation?' Re-allocation of costs can then be traced to specific products – or, indeed, distribution channels or market segments. This is the basis of the Activity Based Costing (ABC) approach (see Chapter 4), which suggests that practically all the company's activities are created to produce, sell and deliver the product to the ultimate customer.

The ABC technique involves (1) identifying the activities associated with each product and the related costs and (2) allocating the group costs to individual products in function of the use of overheads in the process of servicing client X in market Y. By taking the precise amount of costs of labour, distribution, stock investments, shelf and warehouse space, logistics, accounts handling, customer servicing and sustaining activities in the field, an improved picture should emerge of what each customer group, distribution channel and product actually costs.

The ABC approach should be the key catalyst in reformulating the corporate pricing policy. Any change in pricing should take account of complexity of each market and the costs-to-serve: those products or markets that make significant demands on the marketing department and on other support services throughout the organization, should logically bear a higher price tag. Failure to adjust cost factors to reflect the real level of support resource usage – ie accounts receivable effort, after-sales service, in-store promotional activities, customer records' handling at HQ, etc – only penalizes those product areas which absorb proportionately less resources than others.

Improved marketing cost and pricing analysis thus deserve more careful attention by marketing heads, for five main reasons.

- Many marketing costs can be significantly reduced or eliminated as a result of operational and housekeeping changes, like investments in IT to speed up the order process, or identifying non-added-value tasks of a process, system or product.

- Marketing costs (and thus potential cost savings) may be obscured in overhead accounts or otherwise overlooked.
- Resources can be re-deployed to more profitable customer groups who absorb less of the salespeople's time and make fewer demands on other services within the organization; only precise costing of each customer group will reveal such information.
- Improved costing data provides the opportunities of assessing options and asking the question: 'What if product A, or promotional scheme B were to be dropped?'
- More detailed information about the cost base enables the marketing department to assess the potential of selling to new customer groups; cost budgets can be set more accurately and performance targets can be set.
- The 'internal' price companies pay for things done wrong – failure costs – can be highlighted, such as the time products and marketing staff sit waiting without generating revenues.

The bottom line is that marketing management no longer can afford to ignore the fact that every task associated with the customer value-chain, from identifying, developing and sustaining the customer's loyalty, has a specific cost attached to it; there are no free in-house services any more. By reducing the need for certain support resources linked to products, distribution channels or market segments, the marketing function can generate alternative opportunities to improve profitability.

Freed-up resources can either be cut or re-deployed to areas where the potential for incremental sales can be exploited.

By arriving at more accurate information about consumer behaviour and the company's cost base, the marketing department is in a better position to construct more sophisticated pricing policies that discriminate between different categories of customers.

Backward costing systems are misdirected

In recent years, management accountants have suggested that another reason for poor pricing has been the traditional 'backward accounting system', which constructs costing structures for products once the design, testing and production processes have been completed. The accountants feel that it is too late, at this stage, to do anything beyond allocating the costs incurred, as some 90 per cent of the product's total costs have already been committed. This has fundamental implications for pricing.

Japanese corporations, after years of relentless cost pruning, have now shifted their emphasis from backward costing to a 'forward costing' system, which entails working towards a series of target costs. A determined price is established corresponding to a specific production volume. Major marketing expenditures and capital investments are justified on the basis of making the product to sell at a predetermined price. Critics of the forward-costing system assert that it is not as accurate as the backward-costing environment, which has its origins in traditional cost management theory. Japanese corporations brush such concerns aside by saying that the essential point is to get the product to the market fast, where success can be achieved by introducing minor amendments to the item. Under such circumstances, both accountants and marketing people begin to use price as a real marketing component with a distinct focus on revenue-generation. This drives the organization to look less in the rear mirror at what has happened and then attempting to control expenditures already committed; at that stage, the opportunity for manoeuvre is limited and events are largely a *fait accompli*.

THE LAST FEATURE IN IMPROVED MARKETING – SPEED TO IMPROVE

In a highly competitive market environment where most companies have difficulties in differentiating their products, one element now stands out as being critical to competitiveness: speed. Getting ahead today is all about the race to improve. The most obvious manifestation of this is the quest to deliver a product faster from the time to conception to the market. Marketing people have a role here in empowering others within the organization to compress the paper-handling cycles in the office.

One US electronics company now halves the time its finance staff takes to issue an invoice to the customer. Not only does this improve the chances of earlier payment, but also reduces the internal costs. This was done by listing all the steps in the process, figuring out which ones added value that the customer would pay for, and then eliminating almost all of the others.

Another automotive parts manufacturer 're-engineered' its salesforce role to speed things up. Now when a customer requests a price, the specifications are automatically keyed-in to computers as an order by salespeople, rather than being retyped after the quote is confirmed and a product is ordered. The company eliminated working out sales taxes in various regions by programming the computers to calculate them using the postal code. Credit checks were also dispensed with except when orders exceeded previous ones by a certain amount. Globally, the company stripped out over 12 steps out of 20, and now takes only one week from the time of the quote to the shipment.

WILL THE MARKETING FUNCTION SURVIVE?

Given the profound changes occurring in the marketplace, marketing decision-makers should not be in a position where they are tackling challenges of the 21st century with methods and skills of the 20th century. The McKinsey 1993 report on marketing's mid-life crisis asserted that many of today's marketers may not make it.

Some corporations are restructuring their marketing activity to reflect the changing dynamics of the market and placing more emphasis on product innovation. Marketing heads may no longer have responsibility for sales, advertising and promotion; these tasks will be 're-distributed' to the whole organization. Identification, maintenance and retention of the customer's business will become everyone's business in the organization, from the way a customer's billing inquiry is handled by the accounts department to the quality of advice provided by the telesales assistant. It is clear that in a customer-dominated and customer-driven economy, failure to get what they want at the desired price, accompanied by a qualitative level of service they require from the manufacturer or other partner in the value-chain, entices customers take their business elsewhere.

The marketing decision-maker of the future will have to spend more time on product innovation and improvement, constantly re-assessing which brands should be maintained and which should be discontinued. They will also need to re-assess the validity of the other elements in the '4 Ps' – promotion, place and price – and decide which aspects of marketing are more meaningfully handled by corporate HQ and which should be devolved to local business units. Learning from best marketing practices in local business environments or from competitors in other countries will be an important factor in staying on the leading edge of their sector.

Marketing has to be structured as a process rather than a stand-alone function, transforming all parts of the organization into a federation, focused solely on customer development and fulfilment. Customer issues will then be handled anywhere in the organization, rather than being stalled between functional barriers.

KEY ISSUES

■ Customer satisfaction is not sustainable if vast parts of the organization are not capable of contributing to customer development and delivery system fulfilment.

■ Marketing decision-makers need to re-appraise the validity of the '4 Ps' from the customer's perspective: the greater the intensity and diversity of marketing activities in increasingly diversified market segments, the greater the management burden and the risk of customer confusion.

■ Every three years challenge each product, service, promotional activity and distribution channel with the question: 'If the company wasn't in it already, would it be going into it now?'

■ Not all customers are equally valuable to the company; some customers are cash cows, a few are stars, many are question marks and too many may be dogs.

■ Every new customer costs more money to acquire. The more perennial the nature of the customer's relationship with the company, the more that customer is worth: long-term customers buy more, absorb less of the salespeople's time and require less corporate support.

■ Companies need to develop an ongoing plan to retain customers; this requires monitoring outside events, habits, preferences and other customer features that could trigger off defections.

■ Salespeople's time is not always deployed on tasks that are remotely linked to the customer: administrative work, travelling, meetings, etc can be an unproductive deflection of salespeople's time.

■ Review the 80/20 relationship of the business: 80 per cent of business is shared amongst 20 per cent of customers, suggesting differentiating levels of responsibility required to handle big and small customers.

- Own-branding policies can result in cannibalizing the company's main brands and are also a source of hidden and incremental additional costs.
- Selection of the distribution partner must go beyond volume performance: low satisfaction with the retailer selling the company's products quickly translates into low satisfaction with the manufacturer.
- Pricing policies can be improved through a better understanding and reporting of the company's cost base; more sophisticated pricing policies can help to discriminate between different categories of customers.
- Marketing needs to be structured more as a process than a function to ensure that essential customer issues can be handled anywhere in the organization and not be stalled between functional barriers.

BIBLIOGRAPHY

W Bulkeley, 'Pushing the pace', *The Wall Street Journal* (27 December 1994)

D Dayan, 'Des clients sur-mesure', *Le Figaro* économie (13 March 1995)

R Donkin, 'Life after the salesman dies', *Financial Times* (15 August 1997)

P Drucker, 'The theory of business', *Harvard Business Review* (September-October 1994)

The Economist, 'Selling PCs like bananas' (5 October 1996)

The Economist, 'Media-buyers break free' (27 September 1997)

Financial Times, 'Closer to the customers' (7 November 1994)

Financial Times, 'Safeway/BP', The Lex Column (7 September 1996)

D Finkelman and A Goland, 'How not to satisfy your customers', *The McKinsey Quarterly* (Winter 1990)

A Fisher, 'A sharp break with tradition', *Financial Times* (12 August 1996)

J Fredericks and J Salter, 'Beyond customer satisfaction', *AMA Management Review* (May 1995)

A Grant and L Schlesinger, 'Realize your customers' full profit potential', *Harvard Business Review* (September-October 1995)

I Handkan, 'A la conquete du nouveau consommateur', *Le Figaro* (13 March 1995)

O Harari, 'Should internal customers exist?', *AMA Management Review* (July 1991)

O Harari, 'Stop trying to beat your competitors', *AMA Management Review* (September 1994)

V Houlder, 'Knowing when the price is right', *Financial Times* (29 April 1996)

N Inparato and O Harari, 'When new worlds stir', *Management Review* (October 1994)

C Lorenz, 'Competition intensifies in the fast track', *Financial Times* (28 June 1991)

R McKenna, 'Real-time marketing', *Harvard Business Review* (July-August 1995)

C Meeus, 'Géomarketing: un ciblage en trois dimensions', *Le Figaro* (30 October 1995)

A Mitchell, 'A costly presence', *Financial Times* (1 September 1994)

R Narisetti, 'Too many choices: P&G seeing shoppers were being confused overhauls marketing', *The Wall Street Journal* (20 January 1997)

L O'Brien and C Jones, 'Do rewards really create loyalty?', *Harvard Business Review* (May-June 1995)

J Quelch and D Kenny, 'Extend profits not product lines', *Harvard Business Review* (September-October 1994)

F Reichheld, 'Learning from customer defection', *Harvard Business Review* (March-April 1996)

F Reichheld and W Earl Sasser, 'Quality comes to services', *Harvard Business Review* (September-October 1990)

C Romano, 'Death of a salesman', *AMA Management Review* (September 1994)

D Sauzay, 'Conquérir le marché européen', *L'Entreprise*, 127 (April 1996)

D Summers, 'Unloved and incompetent', *Financial Times* (25 August 1994)

D Summers, 'Striving to hit more eyeballs', *Financial Times* (3-4 September 1995)

D Summers, 'When brands face the threat of cannibalism', *Financial Times* (19 March 1996)

The Times, 'Mid-life crisis for TV adverts' (20 September 1995)

M Treschow, 'Electrolux comes under the scalpel', *Financial Times* (29 October 1997)

S Vandermerwe, 'From fragmentation to integration: a conceptual pan-European marketing formula', *European Management Journal*, 7(3)(1989)

J Willman, 'Slimmering symbols of the modern age', *Financial Times* (17 October 1997)

B Wysocki, 'New buzzword sweeps US companies: growth', *Wall Street Journal* (9 December 1996)

Bibliography of material written by David P Doyle

BOOKS

Strategic Management/le Management Strategique, Edition
   Communications Actives (France) (1990), Chapter VIII
Cost Control: a strategic guide, Kogan Page/CIMA (London) (1994
   and 1996), Chapters V and IX.

ARTICLES

'Controlling those marketing costs', *Marketing Opinion* (Ireland)
   (February 1983)
'A different approach to international marketing', *Irish Marketing
   Journal* (June-July 1990)
'Going back to basics in marketing', *Management Accounting*
   (November 1995) 'Satisfying the customer at the right cost',
   Irish Marketing Journal (October 1996)
'Differentiated marketing strategies: a cost nightmare', *MII News*
   (November-December 1996)

CONFERENCES

'Different approaches to markets', paper presented at AMA Top
   Management Forum, Bruges (Belgium) (May 1987)
'Strategic cost control in marketing', paper presented at CIMA
   World Class Financial Management Conference (London)
   (November 1995)
'Controlling costs of the marketing activity', paper presented at
   Ecole Supérieure de Commerce de Paris (France) (October
   1996)

'Planning and executing international mergers & acquisitions', paper presented at HEC-ISA School of Management (France) (November 1997)

Index